BENNACHIE

ALEX INKSON McCONNOCHIE

with a new Foreword and Introduction by
the Bailies of Bennachie

ABERDEENSHIRE CLASSICS

Republished from the original 1890 edition

James G. Bisset Limited
12 Upperkirkgate
Aberdeen
1985

James G. Bisset Limited
12 Upperkirkgate
Aberdeen
AB9 1BG

© James G. Bisset Limited

British Library Cataloguing in Publication Data
McConnochie, Alex Inkson
Bennachie. — (Aberdeenshire Classics)
1. Bennachie (Aberdeenshire) — History
I. Title   II. Series
941.2'32   DA890.B4/

ISBN: 0-948246-02-2

Printed by Fretwell & Cox, Keighley, West Yorkshire

BENNACHIE

Foreword

The Bailies of Bennachie

Copies of Alexander Inkson McConnochie's *Bennachie*, the main source of information on the hill and the surrounding area, have been sought after for many decades. It has therefore given great pleasure to the Council of the Bailies of Bennachie to be invited by James G Bisset to participate in the reprint of this Aberdeenshire classic.

Interest in the hill has always been great but has increased rapidly in recent times, and the extra pressure being put upon it was giving concern. In an effort to preserve the amenities of the area the voluntary conservation society, the Bailies of Bennachie, was formed in 1973 under the enthusiastic leadership of Dr Daniel Gordon, the Founder Senior Bailie.

Briefly, the objectives of the Society are:-

* To preserve the amenity of the hill and to combat litter and vandalism.
* To maintain footpaths and rights of way.
* To study the rocks, plants and animals found on the hill.
* To collect and preserve the literature, including ballads, legends, poetry, prose, as well as art and music, concerned with the hill and surrounding area; also to encourage new writings on the subject.
* To encourage and stimulate public interest in, and care for, the hill.

i

Almost 3000 persons have to date paid the modest life membership fee of £1, and the task of keeping in touch with them in all parts of the world has been undertaken by Mrs Helen Fraser, our indefatigable Clerk.

The Society is under the direction of a Council appointed annually, along with the landowners, and a senior representative of the Forestry Commission. The provision of forest walks, picnic sites, car parks and toilets by the Forestry Commission is much appreciated.

Over and above general maintenance work on the hill undertaken by Bailies with occasional assistance from other groups, considerable research has been, and continues to be, carried out on such subjects as the Colonists and the Maiden Causeway.

The Bailies' publications, including *The Book of Bennachie* and *Bennachie Again*, both with articles by various authors, the excellent *Guide to Bennachie* by James R MacKay, former Senior Bailie, the *Poems of Bennachie* and a detailed map of the hill have all proved very popular.

The love and esteem in which Bennachie is held is shown by the attendance of over 600 members at the Annual Rally and Picnic at the foot of the hill, while the Annual General Meeting is correspondingly well attended.

The Bailies feel that Alexander McConnochie would have approved of their aims and their efforts to fulfil them, and they in turn are very happy to support the reprint of his most informative and readable book.

October 1985   James Kelman and Algy Watson,
                              Senior Bailies of Bennachie

Introduction

Alexander McConnochie: a Biographical Sketch

In 1935, the *Cairngorm Club Journal* published a series
of articles dealing with its past editors. It paid tribute
to one of its founder members, Alexander Inkson
McConnochie, in these terms:

> First secretary of the club and Editor of the *Journal* for
> many years. Tall and athletic, he tramped all the hills
> of our district with perfect intimacy, and his
> knowledge extended over most of the Highlands. In
> the nineties of the last century there was no more
> ardent hill-climber in Scotland, and he was one of the
> first men to climb the higher hills in winter. His
> qualities as a descriptive writer have been very
> frequently seen in the pages of the *Journal,* as well as in
> the series of books which have come from his pen.

The above is an excellent summary of a man of whom
there was very little written, although he was
renowned in his public life by the local press as an
"Aberdeen Celebrity" as early as 1885.

Alexander Inkson McConnochie — author,
accountant, hillsman, naturalist and sporting companion of royalty, was born in Old Street, Rothes on
the 19th February 1850, son of William Inkson, a
local shoemaker, and his wife Jane McConnochie.
He was christened plain Alexander Inkson one
month later. Alex was the eldest of a family of three:
his brother William McConnochie Inkson was born

two years later, followed by his sister Helen in 1856. Helen ultimately married James Innes and moved to Lossiemouth, while William had a butcher's business in Rothes, and later became Provost of the town.

The three children were long lived — Helen died in 1931, and William in 1933 following a road accident : while cycling "down the brae" into Rothes one day, he swerved to avoid a cat and fell off his bicycle. As a result of his injuries he soon became confined to a wheel-chair and died shortly after. Alex, however, outlived them both, dying in 1936 in Cricklewood, London.

Into his 85 years he packed enough to fill several lifetimes of other mortals, and it is interesting to speculate how this "jewel" arose from what seems to be an otherwise "homely" family.

The introduction to *Bennachie* may give us one clue.

> These pages are gratefully dedicated to the memory of Erskine Maitland (born 9th April 1819 — died 7th June 1885) who inspired my boyhood spent with him at the Back o' Bennachie with a love of mountains.

Jane Inkson, Alex's mother, died in 1861, while her family was still young. The family seems to have been separated at this time, and Alex, as the eldest son, was taken into the home of Helen McConnochie, Jane's sister. His father later remarried, and it may be that his adoption by his mother's side of the family inspired Alex to change his name to A. I. McConnochie. Helen McConnochie was married to the afore-mentioned Erskine Maitland — giving us the "Garioch connection", and the reason for *Bennachie's* dedication — for Erskine was the station-master at Inverurie, and both he and Helen are buried in Oyne churchyard. Alex attended Oyne school, and it is easy to imagine him spending his leisure hours on near-by Bennachie, exploring the nooks and crannies, observing the wildlife, hearing the local folk-tales and discovering a love of the hills which was to stay with him all his life. No wonder that in 1890 he produced this erudite volume showing such a vast understanding of the local ways — for in many respects he was a "Garioch loon"!

Scottish Notes and Queries in a review of the work said that: "There seems to be nothing worth knowing about Bennachie that the author has not gathered into this timely volume . . . It [Bennachie] is seen to be invested with a large amount of interest, topographical, legendary and historical . . . We feel sure this volume will be popular".

By 1893, *Scottish Notes and Queries* had been proved correct, the publishers (D. Wyllie & Son) were advertising a "Second Edition (Revised) in Preparation", but this was not printed until 1897 (by Lewis Smith & Son).

Bennachie underwent a number of changes in the second edition, but perhaps the most striking of these is the inclusion of his personal comments on the partition of the Commonty of Bennachie and public access to the hill.

> We do not fear that access to the mountain top will be refused . . . but we do fear that there will be restrictions of free access — that efforts will be made to exclude the public from all parts of the mountain except the mere beaten tracks, and especially from the woods which have been planted around it, and the wide moorlands between the summits. Unless this can be secured for all time coming, under the administration of the Landlords, the duty of the representatives of the

general public of the County and City of Aberdeen is clearly to obtain it by judicial procedure. — What Epping Forest has been made by legislation to the teeming population of the Metropolis, Bennachie should be made to the rapidly increasing community of the Granite City.

These strongly worded statements show Alex to have been a man of considerable vision, having surprisingly advanced ideas on public access to the countryside and mountain conservation. Clearly his views and character had been greatly influenced by his time at the Back o' Bennachie with his adopted family.

Presumably the Maitlands encouraged Alex with his schooling, for he went on to become an apprentice in a law office in Aberdeen, and eventually started business as an accountant and law stationer. Alex was highly successful at his chosen profession, becoming, in 1877, an Associate Member of the Society of Accountants of England, and when this body was merged by Royal Charter into the Institute of Chartered Accountants of England and Wales in 1880, he became an Associate (A.C.A.), but he never attained membership of the Scottish equivalent, possibly due to a lack of the appropriate qualifications.

In spite of his professional success, however, it is for his other interests he is mostly remembered today. In 1888, he was one of the six founders of the Cairngorm Club, a mountaineering and hillwalking club which enjoys a high reputation to this day. They held their first official meet on 9th July 1889 in the Cairngorms, and it is recorded that Alex was responsible for the hot lunch of soup and boiled beef! He was Secretary of the club and Editor of the *Journal* for several years, and in fact wrote many of the articles contained within the pages of the early volumes. Even before the publication of the *Journal*, he was largely responsible for producing the monographs issued prior to club excursions, which contained notes on such subjects as topography, geology and botany.

> Though the moon's on the loch, and the mist's on the hill,
> Though the great giant Bens be enshrouded in snow,
> Though the eagles be screaming and maidens be
>   dreaming,
> Buckle ye, brave hearts; like men, bundle and go.
> Tramp! Tramp! Cameron, McConnochie,
> Tried "Cairngorm Boys", tramp it in order;
> Tramp! Tramp! Copland and Anderson –
> Keep up the name this side of the border!
>
> (*Away to the Hills! Away!* C.C.J. Vol.1)

During the years of his residence in Aberdeen, Alex was a prolific writer — apart from the publication of *Donside, Deeside* (of which it is said that Queen Victoria "graciously accepted" a copy for the Royal Library at Balmoral) and *Bennachie*, he wrote volumes such as *Ben Muich Dhui and his Neighbours* which was originally intended for private circulation, *Lochnagar, Queen Victoria's Highland Home and Vicinity and Views of Speyside*. Of *Lochnagar, Scottish Notes and Queries* writes that . . . "he [McConnochie] knows his subject thoroughly and practically. Hence as guide books, the present, as well as the other volumes, are deserving of every confidence." He was also a Free Mason, co-editing a volume entitled *Craft Freemasonry* with John Crombie.

Alex married a lady artist during this period, and lived in Devonshire Road, Aberdeen, but about 1910 moved his residence to Glasgow. Now in his sixties, he resigned his posts as Secretary and Editor to the Cairngorm Club, but he continued to contribute articles to the Journal for many years. It was in Glasgow that he spent the war years, in the Army Service Corps Office, Maryhill Barracks, where he was a transport clerk of war stores (railway and steamer traffic) from December 1914 to March 1917. From then until December 1918 he worked as assistant cashier (on Government work only) to William Beardmore and Co., Ltd., ordnance manufacturers of Parkhead, Glasgow.

About 1922, Alex moved from Glasgow to London. Although he lived "in exile" from the North-East for the last 26 years of his life, he did not abandon his native parts, making frequent trips back to Aberdeen — a favourite excursion, whilst in town, being to Brown's in Union Street to buy yellow fish (apparently he was always greeted here as a long-lost friend!). He made trips back to his family in Rothes, too, but habitually spent most of his time tramping his beloved hills.

It was during this latter period of his life that he wrote three books on one of his particular hobbies — deer stalking (it is said that he included Edward VII amongst his stalking companions). The *Deer and Deer Forests of Scotland* was published in 1923, *Deer-Stalking in Scotland* in 1924, and *Deer Forest Life* in 1932. Apparently, at the time of his death he was working on another volume, *Birds in Deer Forests*. Also at this time he became a Fellow of the Zoological Society of London, his recommendation being made by none other than the well-known hillsman and naturalist Seton Gordon, on his "personal knowledge".

Alex died in London on January 1936. In William

Garden's *In Memoriam Alexander Inkson McConnochie*, we read that it was a great privilege to be one of his many friends and to accompany him on some memorable tramps. It is, likewise, a great privilege for us to follow his footsteps today.

We would like to express our gratitude to Mrs. Isabel Ritchie of Aberdeen, without whose enthusiastic help and guidance, much of the above research would have been impossible.

October 1985   G. M. L. and M. B. Davidson,
                                                Whiteford

ABERDEENSHIRE CLASSICS

James G. Bisset hope to publish at regular intervals
the following titles in this series:

G. M. FRASER	Aberdeen Street Names
G. M. FRASER	Old Bridge of Dee and Other Essays
JOHN GRANT	Legends of the Braes o' Mar
ALEX McCONNOCHIE	Lochnagar
ALEX McCONNOCHIE	Ben Muich Dhui and his Neighbours
JOHN HILL BURTON	The Cairngorm Mountains
JOHN MACKINTOSH	History of the Valley of the Dee
JOHN GRANT MICHIE	Deeside Tales
G. WALKER	Aberdeen Awa'

Already published, uniform with this edition of BENNACHIE is:
ALEX McCONNOCHIE	Deeside
ALEX McCONNOCHIE	Donside
GAVIN GREIG	Logie o' Buchan

BENNACHIE

BY

ALEX. INKSON McCONNOCHIE

AUTHOR OF "BEN MUICH DHUI AND HIS NEIGHBOURS : A GUIDE
TO THE CAIRNGORM MOUNTAINS"

ABERDEEN

D. WYLLIE & SON

1890

CONTENTS.

		PAGE
CHAPTER	I.—THE HILL,	9
CHAPTER	II.—THE ROUTES TO THE HILL,	18
CHAPTER	III.—ON THE TOPS *(Illustrated)*,	37
CHAPTER	IV.—ITS BALLAD LORE,	61
CHAPTER	V.—THE COMMONTY,	88
CHAPTER	VI.—THE DIVISION OF THE COMMONTY,	98
CHAPTER	VII.—THE MAIDEN STONE *(Illustrated)*,	110
CHAPTER	VIII.—THE GARIOCH,	122
CHAPTER	IX.—THE GADIE,	128
CHAPTER	X.—ITS NEIGHBOURS,	134
CHAPTER	XI.—ITS CASTLES AND MANSIONS *(Illustrated)*,	141
CHAPTER	XII.—ITS GEOLOGY AND BOTANY,	156
CHAPTER	XIII.—THE BATTLE OF HARLAW,	162
	INDEX,	171

BENNACHIE FROM THE SOUTH-EASTWARD.

BENNACHIE.

CHAPTER I.

THE HILL.

Grey king of common hills.

The Mither Tap o' Bennachie,
The sailors' lan'mark frae the sea.

Tap o' Noth an' Bennachie,
Twa lan'marks o' the sea.

Clochnaben an' Bennachie,
Twa lan'marks o' the sea.

There are twa lan'marks o' the sea,
Clochnaben an' Bennachie.

Clochnaben an' Bennachie,
Cairn-mon-earn—a' three
Are lan'marks o' the sea.

When Bennachie pits on its tap,
The Garioch lads will get a drap.

A VERY bold peak surmounting a large mountain-mass, rising abruptly more than a thousand feet above the surrounding country, attracts the attention of the traveller at many points for a distance of about twenty miles between Aberdeen and Huntly. The peak is very conspicuous, and is visible for even a greater distance on the heights over which the ancient highway between these two places runs. It is also notable from many of the hill tops within a radius of thirty to forty miles on the watersheds of the Dee, Don, Deveron, Ythan, and Ugie, throughout the Counties of Aberdeen and Banff, and even from points in several other Counties. The whole mountain has, doubtless, received its Gaelic name from the shape of what is now known as the Mither Tap, the point most particularly noticeable—the Gael, on coming within view of this peak, being instinctively impelled to exclaim *Beinn-na-ciche!* It is the object of the following chapters to detail what is known and has been written about this hill.

There is no mountain in Aberdeenshire—or indeed in the north of Scotland—better known, or more visited than Bennachie. This is easily accounted for. Its graceful outline ; its standing comparatively alone, and being thus discernible and prominent from all points ; the magnificent mountain and lowland views to be obtained from its summits ; and its easiness of access—all contribute to render Bennachie familiarly known even to those who are not given to mountain-climbing. The surrounding district is also of considerable interest, abounding, as it does, in old castles and other notable buildings ; with the Maiden Stone, Maiden Castle, Maiden Causeway, and the Hill Fort—still puzzles to antiquaries ; not to mention the great battlefield of Harlaw. Moreover, its songs and ballads have such a hold that natives of the district, now spread all over the world, can never forget where

> " The Gadie rins
> At the back o' Bennachie."

Situated in the Garioch, between the Don and the

classic Gadie, near the centre of Aberdeenshire, somewhat over twenty miles north-west of the city of
Aberdeen, and extending generally east and west,
Bennachie lies mostly in the Parish of Oyne, its
three principal tops, which form the eastern half of
the mountain, Mither Tap, Craig Shannoch, and Oxen
Craig, being in that parish, while, towards the centre,
Watch Craig forms the meeting-point of the Parishes
of Oyne, Keig, and Premnay. The western half is
divided between Premnay and Keig by Watch Craig,
Hermit Seat, and Black Hill.

There is considerable diversity in the spelling of
Bennachie, but the mode I have adhered to appears
to be the most correct of the modern spellings. In
the Ordnance Survey 25 and 6-inch maps the name
is given as *Beinn-na-ciche*, which, while it doubtless
represents as nearly as possible the ancient Gaelic
form, is not so easily pronounced by the successors of
the Celts who had so named it. For that reason,
perhaps, the one-inch map gives the name as *Bennachie*. In the "Donean Tourist" it is given as
Beinn-na-chie, "Beinn" being the old form of "Ben,"
a mountain. The name has, popularly, almost as
many meanings as spellings, as the following list
shows :

> The Mountain of the Pap.
> The Mountain of Springs.
> The Mountain of the Tap.
> The Mountain of Sight.
> The Mountain of Chie.
> The Mountain of God.
> The Bend-up-high Hill (!)

Chie is said to have been a pagan deity, the god of

the soil or earth, once worshipped in the district.
It is interesting to observe that the name *Chie* is still
found as part of two local names—Pitmachie (the
hollow of Chie), and Putachie (Pit-ach-chie, the hollow
field of Chie) the old name of Castle Forbes. But
there is no doubt that the meaning first given is the
correct one ; compare *A Chioch* and *Coire na Ciche*
on Beinn a' Bhuird. The last meaning in the list is
rather ridiculous, but it appears nevertheless in a well-
known old county map.

The spelling and the meaning being so various one
is not surprised to learn that the exact heights of the
various summits were not generally known, and
that for a long period the Mither Tap, which has been
ascertained by the Ordnance Survey to rank second in
altitude, was believed to be the highest. Indeed, so
strong is the old belief in some that they will not
yield to the authoritative statements from South-
ampton on the subject. The following are the
principal summits, commencing from the east, with
their heights, according to the Ordnance Survey :

			Feet.
Mither Tap,	-	-	1698
Craig Shannoch,	-	-	1600 (about)
Oxen Craig,	-	-	1733
Watch Craig,	-	-	1619
Hermit Seat,	-	-	1564
Black Hill,	-	-	1412

There is also Millstone Hill, a spur which lies southward of the Mither Tap, from which it is distant about
1⅜ miles. Its height is 1340 feet, and it is all in the
Parish of Oyne, lying between the Mither Tap and the
Don. The name is derived from millstones (of red

granite) which were formerly quarried on it; and those acquainted with the Cairngorm district will remember that there is a mountain in Glen Dee called Carn Cloich-mhuilinn, which means the Millstone Hill.

Sometimes, but incorrectly, the Mither Tap is called the Nether Tap, and Oxen Craig is also known as Mither Tap. The first mistake is rather difficult to account for, unless it be from the fact that a little craig immediately to the north of Mither Tap is called Nether Maiden. The name Mither Tap, though evidently not so ancient as the name of the hill itself, shows in what estimation it had at one time been held. It is also known as the East Top, Oxen Craig being the West Top. From east to west Bennachie extends for a distance of about four and a half miles; from north to south about two and a half miles. Its north and south boundaries may generally, and at the same time pretty exactly, be stated as the Gadie and the Don respectively; on the east the road going northward from the Don, opposite Pitfichie Castle, and joining the north road near the junction of the Ury and the Gadie, may be considered the boundary; and on the west the road from the Bridge of Keig to Auchleven, in the Parish of Premnay.

In going over the tops of Bennachie *seriatim* I shall begin with the most easterly. This gives the place of honour to the Mither Tap, a position which it deserves in many ways. Its peaked summit, surrounded by the remains of an old fort, makes it readily distinguishable from all points, and even from the neighbourhood of Aberdeen, the fort being quite visible at that distance. Craignathunder—a high-*sounding*

name, though the craig is of inconsiderable proportions, and not worth the attention of the general
tourist—is the name by which its eastern slope
is known. Then, immediately to the north, is
Nether Maiden, which may be regarded as a little
aiguille of the "Tap." Northwards, about three-
quarters of a mile, are two small craigs, the space
between which is known as Little John's Length,
to the east of which is Stay Know. Nearly three-
quarters of a mile south-west is Garbit Tap, immediately to the south of which is Quarry Hill. Craig
Shannoch is three-quarters of a mile north from the
latter; and little more than the same distance north-
west of the Mither Tap. About three furlongs south-
west of Garbit Tap is Bruntwood Tap. Oxen Craig is
three-quarters of a mile north-west from the latter, and
nearly the same distance south-west of Craig Shannoch.
Little Oxen Craig is below Oxen Craig about three
and a half furlongs west of Craig Shannoch. Moss
Grieve, or Averon Knap as it is often called, is fully a
quarter of a mile east of Oxen Craig. Hummel Craig
is about five furlongs north-north-west of Oxen Craig.
Watch Craig is about five furlongs west-south-west of
the latter. Hermit Seat—so called, it is said, from a
"hermit" who frequented the hill—is the same
distance north-west of Watch Craig. A mile to the
northward of Hermit Seat is the Hill of Tillymuick.
Black Hill is seven furlongs south-west of Hermit
Seat. Bennachie now falls away to the west; a mile
to the north-west of Black Hill being Brackla Hill,
and nearly a mile to the west-south-west Corrie Hill.
The minor heights, on the south side, are Black Knap,
south of Black Hill, between the Don and the

north Donside road; Turf Hill, over two-thirds of a mile south-east of Black Hill; Scarfauld Hill, half a mile further eastward, Shiel Know being its south-western slope; Blackwell Head about five furlongs still further eastward; and Millstone Hill, as already stated, about 1⅜ miles south-south-west of the Mither Tap. Scare Hill and Tillybrack are the south-eastern and south-western slopes respectively of Millstone Hill.

The only tops marked on the one-inch (contour) Ordnance Survey map (Inverurie—sheet 76) are— beginning at the east—Craignathunder, Mither Tap, Millstone Hill, Tillymuick, Hermit Seat, Turf Hill, Black Hill, Brackla Hill, and Corrie Hill. The more important summits omitted are Oxen Craig, Craig Shannoch, and Watch Craig, but these omissions can pretty much be remedied by observing that Craig Shannoch is about the letter R of "Garioch," and within the 1500 feet contour line; Watch Craig is the height marked 1619 feet, at the top of the first N of "Bennachie"; and Oxen Craig is within the 1500 feet contour line, within which is the A of "Bennachie." These omissions explain why Bennachie is marked in most gazetteers and maps as only 1698 feet in height, and in some cases only 1619 feet; even some of Bartholomew's maps giving the latter as the only height.

Having mentioned all the tops, it may be as well to note the burns rising on Bennachie, as the tourist may thereby be assisted in recognising more exactly the position of the different summits. Only one, Birks Burn, is *named* on the one-inch map, but all are *marked*. Rushmill Burn rises between the Mither

Tap and Little John's Length, or more exactly between
the two words, "𝔐𝔞𝔦𝔡𝔢𝔫 𝔠𝔞𝔲𝔰𝔢𝔴𝔞𝔶." The Clachie
(or Clochy) Burn flows eastward between the Mither
Tap and Millstone Hill; the little burn flowing south,
rising east of the final E of "Bennachie," is the
Ginshie Burn. This burn once flowed, by artificial
aid, into Clachie Burn, but now it is said to send all
its water into Birks Burn. But so level is the ground
at the watershed here that one is inclined to think
that one half of the burn flows eastward and the other
half westward, as, indeed, is shown in Mr. Beattie's
map, when the hill was divided among the adjoining
landed proprietors. The burn to the west of the
Ginshie is Garbit Burn. Between these two is Garbit
Tap, below which is Quarry Hill. Still lower is
Pitgaveny, and below Pitgaveny is the How of the
Garbit. West of Garbit Burn is Dalau (or Delaw)
Burn. Between Ginshie and Dalau Burns is Brunt-
wood Tap. West of Dalau Burn is March (or Middle)
Burn; it is the boundary there between the Parishes
of Oyne and Keig. Between it and Dalau Burn is
Blackwell Head, and west of it is Craiglaggan Burn.
Between the latter and March Burn is Scarfauld Hill,
with Shiel Know and Ferney How. The burn to the
west of Turf Hill is the Star Bog Burn; East of Corrie
Hill is Corrie Burn, and south of Brackla Hill is
Brackla Burn. Back Burn (west) and Fore Burn
(east) join near Lickleyhead Castle, flowing from
Black Hill. The Burn of Ryehill rises to the south-
east of Tillymuick, and, before it joins the Gadie at
Bogandy, receives Gillree Burn, which rises more to
the east. Gill Burn (sometimes called Bogie's Burn,
from passing through the farm of Bogend) rises

between Oxen Craig and Craig Shannoch, entering the Gadie close to Oyne Station. This completes the list, and the tourist should now be able to identify the various tops and use an ordinary map without difficulty.

There is a prophecy concerning "the keys of Bennachie," which is attributed to Thomas the Rhymer. It runs thus :

> Scotland will never be rich, be rich,
>   Till they find the keys of Bennachie ;
> They shall be found by a wife's ae son, wi' ae e'e,
>   Aneath a juniper tree.

Another version has it :

> A mither's ae son wi' ae e'e,
> Sall fin' the keys o' Bennachie
> Aneath a rash buss
> I' the backward o' Tullos.

Tullos is to the eastward of the Mither Tap, on the road leading from Blairdaff to Pittodrie. One man is said to have been fortunate enough to find the key sticking in the lock, but as he was unable to turn it he placed his hat on the key to mark the place, and went for help ! But, alas ! on his return, hat, key, and all had disappeared.

CHAPTER II.

THE ROUTES TO THE HILL.

Leaving Aberdeen, Bennachie may be reached by the Great North of Scotland Railway from Pitcaple or Oyne Stations on the main line, or from Kemnay or Monymusk Stations on the Alford Branch. The distances to these stations from Aberdeen are—Pitcaple 21½ miles, Oyne 24¾ miles, Kemnay 18 miles, and Monymusk 21 miles. There is now no "house of entertainment" at Pitcaple, at Oyne there is a public house about half-a-mile east of the station, at Kemnay there is a hotel near the station, and there is also a hotel in the village of Monymusk. The old inn at Pitcaple was long the seat of the Presbytery of the Garioch, as well as the meeting place of the Garioch Justices of the Peace. It is a little over 2 miles as the crow flies from Oyne to Oxen Craig, the highest top ; from Pitcaple, a little over 4 miles ; from Kemnay, about 5½ miles ; and from Monymusk, a little over 5 miles. The distances from these stations to the Mither Tap are, respectively, 2¼, 3¼, 4⅞, and 5 miles.

Whitehouse Station on the Alford branch is not without its advocates as a starting point for the tour of Bennachie's summits. From the station the road is taken northwards to Bridge of Keig, a distance of about 2½ miles ; thence, passing Castle Forbes on the right, the tops may be taken in regular order from the west, landing at Oyne or Pitcaple as may be found most convenient.

FROM OYNE.

Bennachie is seen to advantage shortly after Pitcaple Station is passed, the first summit observed being the Mither Tap. As Oyne is approached that summit disappears, and, at the station itself, the hill has a very graceful outline, fronting, in a manner, the railway. The slope at the now visible eastern extremity is known as "the Brow"; the craggy top next it is Craig Shannoch, west of which is a depression, and then Oxen Craig—the latter with a very unassertive appearance for its rank in the list of summits. West of Oxen Craig is the somewhat flattish top Hermit Seat, beyond which the hill slopes to the west. The hollows formed on the hill are known as "gills," the one nearest the Brow being called the Kirktown (of Oyne) Gill; the one between Craig Shannoch and Oxen Craig is the Westhall Gill; the next is the Gilree or Ryehill Gill; and the most westerly is the Premnay Gill. At the top of the Kirktown Gill is the "Berry Pot," and here, it is said, snow generally lies longer than on any other part of Bennachie; and here also many a sheep in the commonty days has sunk in the bog to rise no more.

Starting from Oyne Station (365 feet) we make for the hill by the cross road that connects the Insch and Huntly turnpikes. This takes us along the Gill Burn, which is crossed a few yards from the railway by the Insch road at a point, as the milestone informs us, 24 miles from Aberdeen. Keeping by the burn we leave the macadamised roads and enter at the bridge on the hill cart-track, for it is so rough that it hardly deserves the name of road. Passing the first farm on the right, Bogend, in a little over half-a-mile we cross the old Aberdeen road, which ran closely along the north foot of the hill. This is the road from Aberdeen to Huntly from the northern end of the Gallowgate, by Kittybrewster, the west side of Woodside, Buxburn, Tyrebagger, Kinellar church, Kintore, the west side of Inverurie, Chapel of Garioch, the Maiden Stone, Bennachie, Insch, &c. It is the road mentioned in the Harlaw ballad :

> As I cam' in by Dunnideer,
> An' doun by Netherha'.

The ground in this neighbourhood has been reclaimed from the hill within the memory of "one of the oldest inhabitants," whose grandfather, along with another farmer, is said to have taken a lease of hill-ground at fourpence per Scottish acre. On going to view their new possession, one of them is said to have exclaimed— "A groat th' yacre ! an' hoo can we pey't ?" "The Three Fords" (462 feet), so called from three small burns meeting here, is situated between the hill road and Masonford (471 feet), now known as Horndoyne— a farm about a hundred yards to the right. Here, it is said, a fierce skirmish took place between the Laird of Harthill—the ruined castle is a mile to the east— and his followers and a party of the Gordons. The latter, by order of their chief, the Earl of Huntly, were conveying to Strathbogie twelve waggon loads of treasure which they had seized at the Cathedral of Old Aberdeen—the period being the time of the Reformation—when Harthill set upon them with the view of intercepting the treasure, and turning it to his own account. However, he was beaten off, and the Gordons succeeded in reaching Strathbogie with the valuables. Bishop Gordon was the Bishop of Aberdeen at this time, and was a near kinsman of the Earl of Huntly. He is believed to have sent the Earl all the silver vessels, which doubtless he duly melted. At Mason-ford also, over a hundred years ago, in the days when " twal-ousen " teams in cart and plough were in vogue, tradition says that a particular team of oxen, before whom a piper, as was customary, played, refused after midnight on a Saturday night to go a step further. Their load, which was lime from Aberdeen, was accordingly emptied there, with the result that the garden of Masonford has the reputation of being particularly fruitful ever since.

One way to the Mither Tap from this point is by taking the old road to the left '(the east) and going round the foot of the Brow, when presently the Tap will come into view with a road all the way. This route dispenses with crossing Bennachie between Oxen Craig and Craig Shannoch, but misses the highest summit. I therefore presume the moun-taineer prefers, as I do, the Oxen Craig route. Lunch, however, may be sent round by this old road to meet the party at " Hosie's Well."

The wooded eminence to the right (west) is Berry Hill (570 feet), on the top of which is the site of a Roman encampment or fort. A circular wall of loose stones now marks the spot.

About half-a-mile west is a mineral well, known as the Hill Well, on the Gilree Burn. To the generation that is now passing away the Hill Well had, in their younger days, a great fascination, especially on the first Sunday of May. Then it was much resorted to by the young men and women of the district, and offerings of coppers and pins were made to it.   There was a superstition that the first person who drank out of it on the first Sunday of May would be lucky above his fellows, so strong being this belief that many have been known to reach the spot on the Saturday night with the view of waiting for a drink of the " cream of the well."   The crofter on whose ground the well was situated seems to have encouraged the popular idea of its medicinal and other virtues, as he frequently cleaned it, more with the view of appropriating the coins at the bottom than of assisting his fellow-creatures.

The crofter added to the scanty fruits of the hard, stony ground—there is a rhyme, by the way, that pretty accurately describes the parish (Oyne) :

> Whan aince ye're intae Een
> Ye're in a gutter or a stane—

by doing a little whisky-distilling in the gully of the Gilree Burn above the well.   In course of time, however, the " sma' still " got so notorious that it had to be given up some time previous to 1853.   Ultimately the "distiller" sunk to the status of a "squatter," keeping a good few score of sheep on Bennachie, but he had a strong belief that an even number was unlucky, and accordingly took care to have *one* sheep more than the number of scores.   He had, of course, to use the "flail" of a morning to thresh out straw for his "beasts," and as showing the then remoteness of the district the following anecdote is related :—A shepherd passed the crofter's one Sunday forenoon, and was rather surprised to see him at work with the flail in the barn.   On asking him why he was at the flail that day he got for answer that he "wis jist threshin' oot some strae for the nowt." "But ye micht tak' anither day than Sunday for that job," replied the shepherd. "Ay, but this is no Sunday," said the thresher. "Hoot, ty, man, it is that; I ken fine it's Sunday, for ilka week day I get porridge to brawkfast an' tay on Sunday, an' I got tay the day," said the simple shepherd. "Weel, weel, maybe ye're richt," was the reply, "but I hae my doots, sae we'll jist awa' in an' look the almanik."

Crossing the Gill Burn, near the Three Fords, we enter on what was formerly the Hill Park of West-hall, now known as the Fir Park of Ryehill. It is said that the laird of Logie-Elphinstone seized it over a hundred years ago, and had it ploughed up. He is reported to have paid his ploughmen a penny a day, with the result, on account of this high pay, that they frequently got drunk on home-brewed ale.

Crossing another small burn, we are, in a few yards further along, at "The Beeches," a group of half-a-dozen fine old beech trees. These trees are believed to have been planted at the same time as the old beeches at Westhall, the young trees having been taken from Monymusk. The Church of Oyne was roofed with timber cut here in 1806. Since then all the wood—with the exception of the beeches—has been cut down, but over twenty years ago Bennachie on this side has been replanted to a considerable height. A little above "The Beeches," to the left, may be seen a field that was formerly known as the Nursery, seedling trees having been reared there for hill planting.

Basil Law, of Ryehill, one of the sawyers employed

at the cutting down of the trees in the beginning of
the century, is said to have been a man of extraordinary strength.   In working an arm-saw that
required two men—one above, the other below—it is
reported that his fellow-workman did not turn up on a
certain occasion.   But Basil mastered the difficulty by
tying a stone to the lower end, and thus working the
saw, pulling *up* saw and stone together, and allowing
the *stone* to take the absent sawyer's place in pulling
down the saw! When the present turnpike from Aberdeen to Huntly was constructed about 1800, a great
many Highlanders were engaged on it.   St. Lawrence
Fair happened to be held as the road was being made
in the neighbourhood of Pitmachie, and, of course, the
Highlanders, to the number of about fifty, threw up
work for the day—as, indeed, was the custom of all,
schoolmasters included, in the district—and went to
the market.   They drank to such an extent that they
were soon quarrelling with all they came in contact
with, and at last, believing in their own prowess and
the reputation they had acquired among the natives,
they resolved to "clear the market."   Very soon there
was a riot, and a messenger was sent on horseback to
Logie-Elphinstone for the Baronet to read the Riot
Act and quell the disturbance.   But meantime Basil
with two stalwart friends set on the fifty Highlanders,
with the result that long before the messenger's
return they were put to flight and peace reigned.   On
another occasion Basil drove a dozen Highlandmen
before him with a stick, and ultimately acquired such
a reputation that the Highlanders fled whenever they
saw him.   "Hoch! it be Basil," has been said by
more than one Gael when the big sawyer unexpectedly

appeared, and with that fleeing incontinently—in more than one instance—to the Hills of Foudland.

As we ascend the road deteriorates, partly on account of the water using it as a channel during heavy rains, and partly on account of having been much used with little repairs spent on it.   So much, indeed, has it been hollowed out that it is now abandoned as a "peat road."   Walking along, we may observe traces of the old low stone dyke that formed the south boundary of the Hill Park.   The trees are pretty close now, sufficiently so to shelter the roe-deer that are sometimes found on Bennachie, and to shut out all view as we ascend.   No less than nine roes have been shot here in one day; and the red deer has been seen, but this is quite an exception.

At the height of about 1050 feet we reach a well, just beyond the trees.   It is on our right as we ascend, and is built around with stone, with seats for the wearied passer-by.   It is often used by tourists and peat-workers, being known to the latter as Shannoch Well.   There is a "short cut" from it on the opposite side of the road down towards "The Beeches."   A little above this well the water in the year '29 cut across the road to the burn below, making a hollow which is yet pointed out.

Passing Shannoch Well we are soon opposite, on our right, Little Oxen Craig, which is worked as a quarry, while on the left is Craig Shannoch.   Between these two tops, in the hollow, is Gill Well, a little above which is the source, among Averons, of the Gill Burn, according to some the best water on Bennachie.   We must now settle what summit we shall take first, and as we naturally give the preference

c

to the highest, we proceed to Oxen Craig. We therefore diverge to our right, making the best of our way by the old peat roads or through the heather.

FROM PITCAPLE.

Pitcaple Station (236 feet), in the parish of Chapel of Garioch, is a favourite point for commencing the ascent of Bennachie, especially the Mither Tap. Leaving the station, the railway is crossed by a bridge, a few yards to the west, and the Parish Church, standing so prominently in view, about a mile to the south-west, at a height of 536 feet, is made for. The inhabitants generally shorten the name of the parish to Chapel. The origin of the name is from the fact of the site of the pre-Reformation church having stood there—the Chapel of the Blessed Virgin of the Garioch, founded before 1357—where Queen Mary is said to have worshipped when she visited Balquhain Castle in the vicinity. The parish as now constituted was formed about 1610 by the union of Logie Durno—which was indeed the old name of the whole parish—Fetternear, and Chapel, the names of the places of worship in the district. The church is passed on the left, when, about half-a-mile westward, the Maiden Stone—which will require a chapter to itself—will be reached. After another half mile the road divides, when the left should be taken. Pittodrie House will be passed on the left, and the hill road, direct for the Mither Tap, is close at hand.

Rushmill Burn, known also as the Pittodrie, or Linn Burn, rising above Hosie's Well, near the Mither Tap, flows past Pittodrie House. A little below the source its flow has been partly diverted, so as to drive the threshing-mill near the house, but the greater part descends in its natural channel, and about half-a-mile south-west of the house, a little above the road among the trees, at a height of about 650 feet, forms a pretty waterfall, having a fall of from 30 to 40 feet. A " fog-house," just below the linn, was built a good few years ago, a little above which may be seen the foundations of the " Bede House," or houses rather, for there are said to have been several of them, very small, each with its own little " yardie." The Bede House " entertained four poor men, who were entitled to a peck of meal, and half-a-peck of malt each, per week ; and who had to wear livery gowns, and to walk to church on Sundays before the [Pitto-drie] family." The last inmates were two women.

In the vicinity of the linn there is believed to have been at one time quite a " clachan," with a small mill and " smiddy," though more than a century ago the buildings had all been allowed to fall into ruins. The name of the burn so far bears out the fact of a mill having been in that neighbourhood, and it may be noted that the burn rises among rushes. It is not generally known, I believe, that the popular song, " My Mither Men't My Auld Breeks," is said to have been written of this "smiddy." The first stanza runs:

> My mither men't my auld breeks,
> An' wow ! but they were duddy,
> And sent me to get Mally shod
> At Robin Tamson's smiddy ;
> The smiddy stands beside the burn
> That wimples through the clachan ;
> I never yet gae by the door
> But aye I fa' a-laughin'.

Near by are the remains of what was once the

house and garden of one Charles Watt, a well-known
Bennachie character. Charlie had the reputation of
being particularly handy at many trades, perhaps,
however, excelling mostly in joinery work. He had
had the misfortune to lose one of his legs, and somehow his appearance inspired not a little terror into the
minds of the youngsters about the vicinity, but,
strangely enough, it was no uncommon sight for his
visitors to see the birds contentedly feeding at table
with him.

About three furlongs north-west of Pittodrie House,
at a height of about 650 feet to the north-east of the
Mither Tap, may yet be seen the remains of Maiden
Castle. It is on the top of a slight rocky eminence,
overlooking, on the north, the old Aberdeen road.
The remains are circular in shape, and on the south
are surrounded by a moat, but on the opposite side no
such protection is required, as the steepness of the
rock had been considered sufficient. The "Castle"
or Fort had been about 90 feet in diameter, and has
now a circle of beech trees growing within the moat,
while the outside is quite surrounded by wood. The
distance to the top of the Mither Tap is about a mile
and a half. The interior of the fort has been dug into,
and pieces of bone and charred wood were found.
The Maiden Causeway had very probably proceeded
from it up Bennachie. In this connection it should
be observed that on the left bank of the Ury, opposite
Pitcaple Castle, are the remains of a circular camp or
fort, near to which the foundations of a bridge across
that river were recently found. Were the Pitcaple
Fort, the Pittodrie (Maiden) Fort, and the Hill Fort
on the Mither Tap part of a chain of Roman Forts?

FROM KEMNAY.

The railway is crossed close to the station, and the Don (264 feet) is also crossed a little to the west. Fetternear House is away to the right (north), and the farm of Greatstone on the left. The "Chapel and Pitcaple" road is entered on the right, nearly opposite Greatstone, passing through Fetternear and Bograxie till the road already designated the eastern boundary of Bennachie is crossed, the tourist then taking the road to the west towards Clachie Burn.

There are several large granite boulders near the village of Kemnay, a particular one being in the glebe, as well as another on the farm of Greatstone which accounts for the name, that were popularly believed to have been hurled by the "aul' Smith" from the top of Bennachie at the priest of Kemnay. This priest was particularly active against Satan and all his works— hence those marks of attention ! The stones are believed by geologists to have been deposited here during the movements of the ice over the country in the glacial period, the principal ones being of the following dimensions :—20 × 12 × 7 feet; 21 × 16 × 8 feet; and the "Devil's Stone" (of which more anon) 20 feet on the incline, 10 feet perpendicular depth, 60 feet in circumference at three feet above the ground, and at five feet up 42 feet. Even Jock o' Bennachie (of whom also more anon) has been blamed for throwing these stones as a pastime while not more seriously engaged with his brother of Noth, but the enemy of mankind ought to get the credit if they were thrown from the Mither Tap, though he is not the only individual who, according to tradition, threw stones from the top of Bennachie.

Sir William Wallace, on a visit to Fetternear, threw a huge boulder from the Mither Tap to the Hill of Barra, near Oldmeldrum. The stone is known as "Wallace's Putting Stone," and lies towards the north side of the hill.

His Satanic Majesty is also fabled to have thrown a stone from Bennachie at his wife (!) in Midmar, but, falling short, it lighted near Tillycairn Castle in Cluny. The incredulous may still see the mark of his hand on it. It is known as the Wolf's Stone, because, as the story goes, a she-wolf had a litter there, and was killed by a woman throwing a girdle at it.

On the north side of Clachie Burn is an old dyke that marks the boundary between the parishes of Chapel of Garioch and Oyne, a little below the farm of Bogheads of Tullos, on the Oyne side of which may be seen a "cup-marked" stone. The stone is of granite, about two and a-half feet square, and ten inches thick. The "cup" is circular, and is five inches in diameter and two inches deep, but slightly raised in the centre of the "cup." There does not appear to be any other marking on the stone. About fifteen yards from the stone, on the other side of the dyke, is a well, now in bad order, known as Kewlie Well. It is also known as the Lady's Well, the laird's wife of Tullos (the old mansion-house may be seen just before the tourist crosses the road to turn westwards) believing so much in its quality that she came there for tea-water. A local shebeener, not so very long ago, used to conceal his smuggled whisky in the neighbourhood of this well.

FROM MONYMUSK.

The outskirts of Bennachie are about four miles

distant from Monymusk Station, so this route is not
so popular as the others.　　The village must first be
reached northward through the wood.　The church is
in the village, a little to the east of which is Monymusk
House.　About a mile north-westward from the village
a road turns to the right (north-eastward), and the
Don is crossed by a ford and ferry, whence the road
past Blairdaff Church is taken till the point where the
tourist turns westward is reached (as from Kemnay).
But preferably, instead of thus crossing the Don, the
village road from Monymusk will be kept for another
mile, passing Pitfichie Castle on the left.　Then the
saw-mill at Ord Mill is reached on the south bank of
the Don, with a corn-mill on the north bank.　The
mills (there was lately a saw-mill as well as a corn-mill)
on the north side are called the Ramstone (or Ramstane)
Mills.　Here there is a foot-bridge across the river
(about 311 feet).

Close to the saw-mill is the entrance to Paradise, a
beautiful spot laid out as a garden and pleasure grounds
in 1719.　There are many fine old larches here that
will attract the visitor's attention.　The proprietor of
Monymusk kindly allows the public the use of the
grounds.

Thomas the Rhymer says that :

> Monymusk shall be a buss
> To draw the dun deer doon.

Buss stands for *busk*, and is considered to refer to the
large number of trees that were planted in the parish.
The "dun deer" *has* been seen in the vicinity, but
that is all.　In some books "buss" is erroneously
printed "busk," as though there was an endeavour to

rhyme with Monymusk, but locally the name of the
parish is pronounced with the *k* mute.

Crossing the foot-bridge at the Mills, the road up
the north bank of the river is taken for about a mile.
The hill-road is entered on just before Upper Woodend is reached on the right, rounding the Millstone
Hill, and at last running parallel to Birks Burn.
Then the Mither Tap is in full view, and should be
easily reached by crossing "Heather Brig" at the
watershed of Birks Burn and Clachie Burn.

If driving, or if the pedestrian has plenty of time on
hand, the tourist may pass Upper Woodend, and the
lodge of Tillyfour House on the left as Oak Brae is
tackled, keeping the north Donside road till Westhaugh, the first farm-steading close to the north side
of the road, is reached. Near Westhaugh, on the
south-west, Birks Burn enters the Don, and on the
east, a cart-road, Bennachie-wards, runs parallel with
Birks Burn, passing on the left the small farms of Mill
of Tillyfour and Tillybrack, and leading upwards to
"Heather Brig." Just before the tourist turns eastward at Westhaugh, "My Lord's Throat," a road in a
deep gorge, may be observed a little further up the
Don. Formerly the tops on both sides of this road
were wooded, but now the trees on the north side
have been cut down.

On the west, as Monymusk Station is left for the
village, is the farm of Tombeg. Here the last of the
Highland "caterans" that ever troubled the parish
made a descent, but were caught and made an example
of. They had ordered the "cow-baillie" to drive all
the cattle out of the byres, but the faithful servant,
while he obeyed the reivers' orders, took care to

knock out a few "sods" in the back wall as he unbound the cattle. Just as he drove out the last he fled through the hole to the laird's, and the result was that the cattle-lifters were overtaken and several of them duly "justiced."

The following little anecdote has been frequently told, but generally applied to other persons than the one actually concerned :—A clergyman from a neighbouring parish, whose memory, from his kindly actions, is yet green among his parishioners, was much more Celtic than Saxon, as his speech shewed. On this particular occasion he was officiating in Monymusk pulpit, and had occasion to come over more than once the names of Shadrach, Meshach, and Abednego. His peculiar pronunciation of these names tickled his hearers so much that at last their smiles became apparent to the Gael, who leaped the ditch later on by referring to "them three goot lats" ! This same clergyman was not without a superstitious tinge, and more than once has told of having seen "phantom" funerals. Convoying a brother priest, he gave him graphic particulars of the appearance of a phantom coffin and mourners he had seen in full procession for —— Churchyard, and then left his friend at the woods of Pittodrie, saying, "But *you'll* not be frightened, Mr ——!" On another occasion he passed the precipitous, almost overhanging, rocks on the left bank of the Spey at Craigellachie Bridge, and actually ran, as he said himself, in case they should fall on him !

Near Monymusk House, there is a stone in the Don known as "Maggie Aiken's Stane," which, when the river is in flood, is covered by the water. The story goes that Maggie was brought before the

laird for stealing a peck of meal, and was condemned
to be drowned in the Don.   The sentence was duly
carried out, and as the poor victim endeavoured to
escape death by clutching this stone, those on the
bank struck at her hands, so that she had to lose her
hold, and was drowned.   Even yet some can see
blood on the stone !

On the opposite side of the Don from Monymusk
House is the farm of Enzian.   About a hundred years
ago the folks there attained notoriety by working on
Sunday "at the flail," plucking live poultry, and sending
them, it is said, "to meet the kirk folk," besides other
cruelties culminating in skinning a live calf.   The
poor brute ran round the corn-yard, and rubbed itself
against a particular rick in its agony.   This was the
last of such devilish pranks, for a judgment, as was
then believed in the parish, overtook those implicated.
The kiln took fire with two men in it, who had taken
a considerable part in these cruelties.   A third, one of
the ringleaders, as he was about to go on the roof with
the view of putting out the fire, was remonstrated with,
but he replied that though it was "as het as the
bran'ers o' hell" he would go.   He went accordingly,
and fell through the roof, and the three men were
burned to death.   One of them before his death is
reported to have rubbed himself against the rick, as
the calf had done.

Formerly there was a meal-mill at Ord Mill, but the
last miller, about 1810, would not work at night alone,
as he fancied he saw a man shaking a bone at him
over the sacks.   Indeed, the surrounding district was
comparatively recently much given to superstitious
ideas.   One man, a carpenter, as he lay in bed in his

master's house, heard saw and planes at work in the adjoining workshop, but on at once getting up to see what was ado, nothing was to be seen and everything was quiet, but next morning there was an order for two coffins! More than one person also heard coffins being made at night before there were tenants ready for them, but they were not in such circumstances long wanting. And naturally, corpse candles would be seen proceeding from the door of the doomed to the churchyard. The writer has been told of such things as veritable circumstances by a Monymusk residenter, who, otherwise common-sense, was an eye-witness of corpse candles, and an ear-witness of mysterious coffin-making noises.

On the north side of the Don, a little to the south of Ramstone Mills, is Lord Cullen's school. It is so named after Sir Francis Grant of Cullen, the first Grant of Monymusk, who assumed the title of Lord Cullen on being raised to the bench. He left an endowment, for educational purposes, of two chalders of meal yearly. A few yards east of the school is Chapelcrook, where are the remains of an old chapel, dedicated to St. Finnan, with a small burying-ground surrounded by trees. It is over a century since the last interment was made here, and as weeds and stones are now deposited in the churchyard there is little or no trace left of its original purpose.

As Woodend is approached from Ramstone Mills a particularly large oak tree may be seen between the road and the river. Here a ghost yet walks, between Saturday and Sunday, dressed in a red cloak. It seems that, in 1818, the then tenant had but an indifferent reputation, having been one of the famed

Gillespie the gauger's gang. A " pack-wife," who was accounted rich for her station, and who generally wore a red cloak, had got leave to spend the night on his kitchen floor, but when all was quiet the farmer got up and killed the "pack-wife" for the sake of her money. The herd-boy was wakened by the noise, and, on seeing the ghastly spectacle, fled across the Don to Milldowrie. In the morning search was made for the murderer, but he and his wife had fled, and were never caught. The victim was buried below this oak tree—hence the ghost.

After leaving Westhaugh behind, Mill of Tillyfour is the first place passed. It is on the left, and derives its name from a meal mill having been there some hundred years ago. It was so small that it is said two dogs could have "licked up" the meal as fast as it was ground !

CHAPTER III.

ON THE TOPS.

I now ask the reader to imagine himself on the summit, and I shall proceed to speak of the more important tops, and tell what is notable or known of them. A single day will suffice for the tourist, and even give plenty of time for going over the most interesting tops. Indeed, a run can be made by starting from Aberdeen with the first afternoon train. But such diligence is not to be commended ; only the fact is mentioned to show Aberdonians how near Bennachie is to them, and how easy the ascent is. A long day can be spent with pleasure ; in such a case one can cross from the Gadie to the Don, or *vice versa*, but the excursion may be diversified and modified to any extent to suit the convenience of parties. There can be no difficulty, except in mist, in finding one's way from top to top, for the distances are so short and the tops so distinct that it is almost impossible to lose the way. At the same time it is but right to say that it is quite possible for a stranger to lose his way on Bennachie in a mist, for such was almost the fate of the writer on one occasion !

The following table shows the distance of the *sea* horizon when seen from various elevations of the land above the sea level as deduced from the size and shape of the earth, and will meet the requirements of the ordinary mountaineer

Altitude above sea, in feet.	Distance of sea horizon, in miles.	Altitude above sea, in feet.	Distance of sea horizon, in miles.
100	13	1000	42
150	16	1250	47
200	19	1500	51
300	23	1750	55
400	26	2000	59
500	30	2500	66
600	32	3000	72
700	35	3500	78
800	37	4000	84
900	40	4400	88

One-fourteenth of an arc has been allowed for refraction, and fractions have been omitted.

Extraordinary distances may, however, in certain states of the atmosphere, be seen. On 21st June, 1819, on the top of Corryhabbie (2563 feet), a mountain in Banffshire at the head of Glen Fiddich, after a stormy day the clouds suddenly broke away about seven o'clock in the evening. At eight o'clock, *under very peculiar circumstances of refraction of the atmosphere in raising objects*, the officers there engaged in the Ordnance Survey saw, through the telescope, a brig under sail to the northward, at a distance which they considered could not be less than 100 miles. The officer in charge was Captain Colby, afterwards Major-General and the head of the Ordnance Survey Department, so the estimation of the distance may be relied on. Elevated land, also, can be seen to a greater distance in an open country, while at the same time a low hill near the observer will often shut out the distant prospect. The greatest distance seen in the United Kingdom, in the Ordnance Trigonometrical Survey, is from Slieve Donard in Ireland to Sea Fell in England, a distance of 111·2 miles.

The following rule, which gives results very near the truth, will be found useful in deducing elevations from aneroids without mountain scales. On the Grampians a depression of four inches gives an elevation of about 4000 feet :

As the *sum* of the readings of the aneroid is to their *difference*, so is 55,000 (or twice the assumed height of the atmosphere in feet) to the elevation required. Example :—

Reading at A...	30·05	30·05	
„ B...	29·44	29·44	
Sum ...	59·49	0·61	Difference.

Ins.　In.　Ft.　Ft.

$\therefore 59·49 : 0·61 :: 55,000 : 565$ nearly.

OXEN CRAIG.

This, the highest point of Bennachie, is a craggy eminence, though not so very much so as others of the tops. The origin of the name cannot now be ascertained, and the writer, after all due inquiry, is unable to hazard even a guess. Locally, it is familiarly known as the *Ousen* Craig. The Bennachie rocks appear in many parts as if systematically piled up, one above the other, in rather a workman-like manner, so that the Highlander who remarked that the masons had been at work here may be forgiven for his mistake. There is a mass of loose stones on the Craig rather roughly thrown together as a rude sort of shelter for quarriers and peat-workers. The cairn erected by the Royal Engineers has succumbed a good deal, owing doubtless to the rough treatment it has received from visitors. The same process of cairn-demolition is found going on upon other hills, but so perverse is a certain class of tourists that it is almost useless to say, "Spare the cairns!" Several small cavities on the rocks may be seen, the rain-water in which is said to be a sovereign cure for warts!

The view from Oxen Craig is by far the grandest and the most extensive to be had from any of the tops of Bennachie. It includes the upper part of the district of the Garioch, bounded on the north by the Foudland Hills, and on the south by the westward continuation of the ridge of the hill itself onward to the Correen Hills; the Vale of Alford, a flat basin to the south-west, encircled by the hills of Cairn William, Corrennie, Callievar, and the western extension of Bennachie, through which the Don winds on to the romantic well-wooded hollow, where it continues its course between Cairn William and Bennachie, from Castle Forbes, past Paradise, to Monymusk; and in the remote horizon to the south-west, west, and north-west most of the highest Aberdeenshire and Banffshire mountains, encircling the upper parts of the valleys of the rivers Dee, Don, and Deveron. The more distant mountain prospect comprises Hill of Fare, Kerloch, Clochnaben, Mount Battock, Mount Keen, Lochnagar, Morven, Ben Avon, Ben Muich Dhui, Cairngorm, Buck of Cabrach, Corryhabbie Hill, Ben Rinnes, Tap o' Noth, Ben Aigan, Knock, Mormond, and Dudwick, and even over the Foudland Hills, and across the Moray Firth, to mountains in Caithness—a distance of about 77 miles. Several minor heights in the immediate vicinity—Hart Hill, Parnassus, Candle Hill, Dunnideer, and Christ's Kirk

Hill—are, along with Cairn William, particularly described in a later chapter. It may be of assistance to the tourist to mention that Buck of Cabrach (17 miles) is almost due west, and Clochnaben (22 miles)—so readily recognisable from its rocky protuberance—is a little to the west of south. To the north and east the landscape is very pleasant, though, of course, differing exceedingly from the mountain views westward looking up the Don towards its source and beyond to the Cairngorms. The view of Lochnagar is particularly fine—but, indeed, from the open situation of Bennachie, already alluded to, the prospect all round cannot fail to be interesting. Something even may be said for the view on a misty morning! On such occasions the prospect will be much enjoyed, for all the lower parts around will be completely mist-clad, while only the hill-tops will be visible like so many islands in a sea.

Oxen Craig has acquired quite a local history—and almost even a name, for sometimes it is spoken of as "Robbie Deson's Tap"—from a half-witted pauper, Robert Dawson, who was found dead on the Craig on 12th December, 1856, the sixteenth day after he had disappeared. Robbie lived with his mother at Gooseknowe, near Ryehill, Oyne, and was last seen alive at Hillbrae. He had left Hillbrae on the 26th of the previous month, a snow-storm coming on rather unexpectedly after he had set out. Search parties were sent out after some delay, but no trace of poor Robbie could be found—indeed, it could hardly be expected that it would have been thought possible or probable that the body would be found on the highest point of Bennachie. Ultimately, the body was found by a

young man of the district who was out "takin' a shot"
at the white hares in the neighbourhood of Oxen
Craig. Robbie had died while sitting on the Craig,
so at first the "sportsman" took the dead body for
some one watching his movements. The crows had
picked out the right eye before the body was found,
which was buried at night in Oyne Churchyard. The
natives erected a commemorative stone, with an inscription, on the spot where the body was found, the stone
being cut from the rock in the immediate vicinity.
Robbie's mother, however, knocked it down and
broke it into minute pieces, her idea being that she
should have participated in the funds that were raised
for its erection. She also objected to the word
"fatuous" on the stone referring to Robbie, saying
" Fatuous ! Fat's that ? My sin wis jist as Guid made
'im." Ultimately the subscription became the subject
of a lawsuit. To use rather an Irish bull—all that
remains of the monument is the square-cut foundation
for the stone in the solid rock, which may still be seen
a few yards from the cairn. Poor Robbie was a
great simpleton. On one occasion he saw a number
of egg-boxes standing on end at the local " grocer's,"
and having been told they were coffins, ever afterwards
he would rather have waded the Gadie than passed
" the grocer's," especially at night.

WATCH CRAIG.

The only top westward of Oxen Craig that the
tourist need care for visiting is Watch Craig, about
five furlongs off, which, as already mentioned, is the
meeting point of three Parishes—Oyne, Premnay, and
Keig. The letters A.P.P. cut on the rock refer to the

plan of the division of the Commonty of Bennachie (detailed in Chapter VI.), and mark the boundary here between the portions allotted to Ardoyne and Auchindoir. The origin of the name of this Craig is also unknown, but it may fairly be presumed to have been so called from having in olden times been used for watching and signalling the approach of the enemy. Between it and Oxen Craig the ground, which descends to the level of about 1400 feet, is bare and gravelly, but recently was all covered with peat. On a blowy day, in very dry weather, it is rather unpleasant walking in this neighbourhood, from the finely powdered remains of the moss entering eyes and ears. Hazel, it may be mentioned, was the wood chiefly found in the moss.

Over forty years ago the body of a woman was found in the moss by the peat-workers, partly devoured by, it is supposed, dogs. It had lain there for a period of about a hundred years, and exemplified one of the peculiarities of the age. The deceased (whose name was Laing) committed suicide in a meal girnal, and was interred in Keig Churchyard. But of course it hurt the feelings of the natives that a suicide should rest in hallowed ground, so accordingly next morning the husband found the body outside his door. He once more tried to get her interred, this time in Premnay Churchyard, but the Premnay folks also objected to christian burial for a suicide, so ultimately a midnight start was made for Oyne. But the burden was too much for the few mourners, and daylight overtaking them, and knowing that an unobserved burial in a churchyard was now hopeless, they interred the body, wrapped in a home-made checked plaid, in the moss.

The circumstances of the burial were carried down to succeeding generations, and, as the moss was gradually converted into peats, the finding of the body was not unexpected. Both corpse and plaid were in a very good state of preservation, through the anti-septic action of the moss, the body being quite plump and mulatto-coloured. The same evening the body, much wasted through exposure to the air, was interred in the Churchyard of Oyne.

The horn of an ox was found here at a depth of about five feet in the moss. Not a few articles of antiquity have also been found in the neighbourhood, half-a-dozen of which are now in the Antiquarian Museum, Edinburgh. These latter consist of a stone-ball, an urn, two cup-shaped urns, a bronze sickle, and a flanged celt. Several ancient coins have also been found.

The best view from this Craig is Don-wards. It is well seen from the Don side, but from the Oyne (north) side it is not visible.

CRAIG SHANNOCH.

Let us now proceed to Craig Shannoch. It has rather an imposing and mountain-like shape from below, but it shrinks somewhat as it is approached. The crags stretch downwards towards Oyne Station for nearly a quarter of a mile, the stones having the same shelving, built-up, masonry-like appearance as those of the highest top. The name denotes the Foxes' Craig, and is quite descriptive of what it once was, for foxes abounded amongst the rocks till quite a recent period. Indeed, in olden times, the complaint was that Bennachie was greatly infested with foxes. While the crags

are not sufficiently high to induce the eagle now to
build on them, the more homely hawk at times has its
nest there. Formerly, however, an eagle built here
on several occasions, but was ultimately captured.
Hares, white in winter, are often to be found round
about the top, the fine and closely-cropped heather
showing where they feed. On the north side, about
half-way down the rocks, is Harthill's Cave, or, as it is
sometimes called, Leith's House. It is a cave formed
by one of the shelving rocks, the space covered by
the overhanging rock being large enough to afford
shelter to two or three persons. The entrance is
rather low, so one has to stoop on entering, and hence
it may be readily passed as one *descends*. It not
unfrequently affords shelter to workers in the moss
when a sudden storm attacks them on the hill. The
cave derives its name from the fact that when Harthill
Castle was burned by the laird, Leith, who had fallen
out with his neighbours (some say because he was
little better than a robber), he fled to Bennachie and
watched it burning from this cave while he himself
was concealed. At that time the mouth of the cave
had not been so open as it is now. One tradition
says that his dog was the means of his being discovered,
but another account states that after setting fire to his
castle he at once fled the country, only to end his days
in the King's Bench, London.

Some thirteen years ago a split was made in the
rock by lightning, the mark of which may still be
seen. At the north end of the crags there is a spring,
and on the west of the south end is, as already
mentioned, the Averon-clothed Gill Well. The latter
is a favourite spot for luncheon, both with sportsmen

and tourists. " Jock's Sark " (see following chapter)
may be observed to the east of the well.

MOSS GRIEVE.

Moss Grieve, or Averon Knap as it is often called,
is here mentioned, not on account of its being worthy
of a special visit, but from the peculiarity of its
names, and its lying almost in the way between the
last two tops. This "top" is a slightly raised
elevation of rock and heather, which had at one time
been completely surrounded by moss, which it had
overlooked, and thus, likely enough, got the name,
facetiously, of the Moss Grieve. In former times
peat-workers have been known to sleep on it over
night, so as to save time and the labour of descending
and ascending the hill. The other name, Averon
Knap, is easily accounted for—that plant (*Rubus
Chamæmorus*, mountain bramble, or cloud berry)
having been plentiful (and is yet, to a certain extent)
all round.

MITHER TAP.

We now proceed to the Mither Tap, nearly a mile
south-east of Craig Shannoch. The ground sinks to a
height of 1418 feet between these two summits.

This is the popular top—the Mecca of Bennachie—
and is visited by thousands annually. Indeed, though
not the highest, it is the most interesting in many ways.
It stands out alone, distinct and prominent, from the
other tops, presenting a pretty steep slope on the east
and south, on which sides it is planted with trees to a .
height of about 1400 feet. The ascent, however, is
very easy and gradual on its other sides. It is also more
peaked, its summit being a huge mass of rock, with a

little spur, Nether Maiden, a few yards to the north. It has a very majestic appearance from the north, east and south, and near or far, is *the* feature of the hill. It was formerly surmounted by a cairn (erected by the Royal Engineers), but all traces of it have disappeared. The "Tap" may be seen from Cat Cairn and Baron's Cairn in Nigg, and from the Blue Hill in Banchory-Devenick.

These natural physical features render the Mither Tap interesting, but an artificial peculiarity about it makes it still more worthy of notice—the great mass of stones that encircles the summit like a fortification. Evidently from the nature and disposition of these stones they have been brought from the neighbourhood and regularly set up by human hands, but by whom and when is unknown. Naturally the Picts—and probably deservedly—get the credit of the building. On one of the sides an entrance has been left in the artificial wall, and at another place there is a well with several steps down to it. The fortification has also been attributed to Sir Andrew Leslie of Balquhain, the Earl of Mar's "master of horse," who fought and was killed at the Battle of Harlaw. Tradition has it that at one time he lived on the top, and carried off young women to this rude fortress, as well as took shelter there himself when his lawlessness put him in disgrace with his superior. But there are several reasons why this tradition should not be credited, besides the absurd account which it gives as to the origin of the Maiden Causeway :—"One of the Lesleys of Balquhoyn, who loved to indulge himself freely in his pleasures, to enjoy them in more security built a strong dyke round the highest top of Bennachie, and, because the passage to it lay through a great moss, he built a long causey through the moss up to the fort, whither he brought such handsome girles whom he fancied, and could forcibly carry away from their parents and friends, defending himself by means of this fort and straitness of the place against such as pursued after him to recover their ravished relations." There is another, and much later, tradition that the fortress was used as a hiding-place, in common with Craig Shannoch, by Lord Pitsligo after he had been attainted for his share in the rebellion of '45. An active search was made for him after the Battle of Culloden, but he always contrived, though often very narrowly, to evade his pursuers. For years he had to lead a wandering life, but ultimately, the Government having given up the pursuit, he died in bed in 1762—one of nature's noblemen. When on Bennachie he occasionally visited his friend General Horn at Logie-Elphinstone, and had a night's hard drinking with him. On the General's wife remonstrating with him against this habit, Lord Pitsligo replied that, "if she was sittin' upon a cauld, bare stane up on Bennachie wi' naething but burn water, she micht ca' that 'hard drinkin'.'"

The well is now dry, the water having disappeared, it is said, in a single night, though some years ago it gave a fair supply of excellent water. At one time it was filled up with stones, to the disgust of the natives, by a crofter-squatter, already referred to, who was annoyed by his sheep wandering to the top of the Mither Tap, and occasionally falling into the well. The stones have since been partly removed, but water appears to have forsaken the place.

The rock on the top is disfigured by visitors who

have left their "mark" behind them cut out on the rock; but there is besides a peculiar inscription which will be found described in Chapter VI.

Nether Maiden, immediately to the north, will not of course escape the visitor's attention. It is a mass of rock that at a distance gives a hump-like appearance to the "Tap," and is seen a long way off. Some contend that the correct name of this rock is Maiden Craig. Formerly a raven used to build on it.

The Mither Tap affords the best view of the lower part of the Garioch towards Old Meldrum and Inverurie in the east; the richly wooded lower part of the valley of the Don to the south-east, with the Kemnay Granite Quarries, onward to the Tyrebagger and Brimmond Hills, beyond which may be seen the smoke of Aberdeen; and a little to the right the Loch of Skene, and the Kincardineshire hills to the south of the Dee. The mountains in the upper regions of the Dee and the Don may also be seen, but the best view of these, and other distant summits, is to be had from Oxen Craig. On a clear day the German Ocean may be seen near the mouth of the Ythan, as well as the Moray Firth off Portsoy and Cullen. Having enjoyed the prospect in full, the mountaineer may descend from the rocky summit within the fortification, and have a little refreshment; but if his lunch is of superior style there is a highly-convenient spot for pic-nicing at Hosie's Well, half-a-mile north from the Tap, close by the wayside. A party of tourist-mountaineers cannot do better than, bringing their own supplies with them, engage a cart from any of the neighbouring farms, and get the pic-nic materials conveyed up to Hosie's Well, which is at a height of 1300 feet, near the top of the Pittodrie Gill, and close to the source of Rushmill Burn. The tourist who goes to the Mither Tap from Pitcaple, or Oyne by the foot of "the Brow," will pass the well on the way up. Who Hosie was has not been handed down by tradition—nothing but the name and the well remain.

Some fifty years ago one William Gilmore built himself a hut there, the remains of which are yet visible, close to the well, and lived in it with his family for about two years. William was wretchedly poor, poverty alone driving him to such a habitation; but he added to his income by selling *aqua*, smuggled, it is feared, to the passers-by, not so numerous then as now, being mostly peat-workers. Ultimately, his case got so desperate that his friends pulled down the house, and removed the occupants to better quarters at Braeside of Pittodrie. The water is of the purest quality, and is properly appreciated by sportsmen and tourists alike. The former make Hosie's Well a *rendezvous*, and many a pleasant luncheon has been discussed there about "the Twelfth," and tourists also have long ago found out the suitability of the place for refreshing the inner man. Altogether, it is an oasis of the desert, a green spot where one can rest and refresh, and gratify the eye with a delightful and magnificent range of scenery. Both hill and dale may be seen, corn-fields and woodlands, and far away the German Ocean, ships being visible with the naked eye in clear weather, and a fleet of herring boats during the season is not altogether an unfrequent sight.

A Dorlethen suicide—(Dorlethen farm is a little to the

south of Pittodrie House)—was duly taken to Bennachie for interment. But a local physician, hearing of
this, had the body taken up for anatomical purposes,
removing it himself on horseback. Landing at a
neighbouring inn he got the use of a big copper kettle
for skeletonising his "subject," but when the landlady
ascertained for what purpose her kettle had been used,
she indignantly broke it up and sold it to "the
tinklers"! The last of these hill burials was that of
a Jane Jack, some sixty years ago. Driven by unkind
treatment, she drowned herself in the Gadie, near
Harthill, and her body was taken to Bennachie, and
buried near Hosie's Well. But the more intelligent
residenters would not allow this, and accordingly the
body was removed and interred in Oyne Churchyard.

Looking at the Ordnance maps the tourist will
expect to have no difficulty in recognising the Maiden
Causeway. There it is laid down with a distinctness
that is not to be met with on the ground, and the
casual observer will in all probability pass it by
unnoticed. The "Causeway" stretches from the
Tap, down to and across the head of Rushmill Burn,
past (a little below) Hosie's Well, on to Stay Know,
and into the Pittodrie woods, where it vanishes from
mortal ken. The road is roughly paved with stones, and
was much more distinct some fifty years ago than now,
the breadth being 14 feet, and is generally believed to
be of Roman origin. One authority, however, con-
tends that its breadth is against its antiquity, and
thinks it probable that it had been made to remove,
for building purposes, the stones of the fort. As to
the origin of the word "Maiden," in the present
instance, it is thought that it is the old past-participle

of the verb "to make," Chaucer often giving the past tense of "make" as "maden." Chalmers in his *Caledonia* says this ancient road is known by the "appropriate" name of the *Maiden Causeway*, it being thus implied that it was not a "track" but a well-"made" road. It has also to be observed that several similar roads in the north of England are known by the same name. "Maiden" is also said to mean, in the connection used here, first.

THE HILL FORT.

The Hill Fort on the Mither Tap is a remarkable structure, rough certainly, but evidently formed from design, and with a great object in view. It well illustrates the refuges or strongholds of the pre-historic inhabitants of the country, erected on defensible eminences, and composed of earth or stones, or of both, the structure being in some cases vitrified. It is described at considerable length by Miss Christian Maclagan in her "Hill Forts, &c., of Ancient Scotland," published in Edinburgh in 1875. Perhaps Miss Maclagan sees more in her subject generally, and on Bennachie, than most of us can perceive, but as she is an authority on Hill Forts, I do not hesitate to use her work in the following description, which has been condensed and abridged from it.

This Hill Fort, of which the sketch on the following page, is from a drawing by the late Mr. Andrew Gibb, F.S.A. Scot., is indeed a vast and singular structure. Still more singular are the peculiar forms of the "munitions of rocks," upon and among which it is "mixed and mingled" as a bird's nest is entwined among the branches of a tree. As the rocky cliff is so narrow, one looks down on the wide expanse, as if

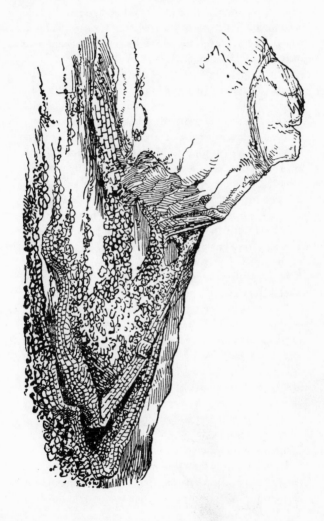

from the "dizzy mast"; a wolf could scarcely have
crept from one thicket to another unseen by the
watchman aloft, and as its elevation is only 1698 feet
above the sea-level, the distance lends enchantment
without adding dimness to the view.

The upper cliffs of the hill are composed of vast
stacks of granite rock, separated from each other by
chasms, whose sides are almost as perpendicular and
squarely cut as the walls of a house. Each of these
chasms or chambers, as it were, is enclosed by these
stacks of rock on three of their sides, and their fourth
now stands open, though it also had been formerly
shut in by a huge wall, broad and lofty, if we may be
allowed to judge of it by the wide area over which its
debris has spread, and by one small portion which
still exists, and is about ten feet in height. These
chasms being enclosed in this manner, and no doubt
at the same time solidly roofed, we can comprehend
how even these storm-beaten mountain peaks may
have been rendered habitable to a hardy race of men.

The area of the summit is 100 feet by 70, and is
deeply indented by these chasms. Around this summit area there is no trace of any wall. The cliffs, or
stacks of rock, which form the summit, are 60 and 70
feet in height. Lower down the sides of the hill there
are several such detached stacks. some of them of
singular mass and shape, and it is among these that
the second and chief wall of the fortress has its course.
Stretching from cliff to cliff, it surrounds the whole
mountain top in a circuit of about 1500 feet.

Here and there its traces are almost obliterated, but
this is only in short spaces. These brief blanks occur
at portions of the circumference where the slope of

the hillside is steepest, and generally one can still see
its ruins scattered below. Within the memory of the
present generation considerable difference has been
made on the appearance of the fort by stones falling
down naturally, as well as being rolled down by
tourists.

The north-east portion of this wall is the most entire,
resting upon a natural terrace level. The semi-
circular sweep of this terrace, with its enormous wall,
is 600 feet, and its greatest breadth is 26 feet; the
entire space seems to have been closely filled up with
buildings. At both ends this terrace gradually narrows
in upon the hill. The one is terminated by one of
the stacks of rock, the other by a steep precipice.

The huge wall or bulwark of stone which encloses
this terrace-level is, like itself, narrowest at its two ends.
There it is about 15 feet in thickness, but in by far the
greater part of its course it is 24 feet, and in some
portions even as much as 26. The wall, at its highest
part, is still probably 14 feet in height, but the vast
accumulation of its own ruins at its base makes it
difficult justly to estimate its true height.

Near the middle of the masonry of this wall there is
the face of an inner wall. Some would term it a
banquette, but probably it is one of the side-walls of
what had been a gallery or chamber in the wall, after
the manner so common in Brochs. And in a wall so
broad as this one we might expect to find galleries of
communication.

The stones of which this wall is composed average
in size 18 inches by 12, and they are all oblong in
shape. Few boulder-like stones occur among the
mighty mass; so uniformly are they angular that

one might be induced to believe that they had all been shaped by human art. We must, however, take into account that this seems to be due to the natural cleavage of the granite rock of which it consists, but still there remain traces of the hand of man upon them.

The masonry is everywhere laid with satisfactory regularity. The hill being very steep outside this wall, its ruins have fallen far below, the largest stones the greatest distances.

In some places the down-pour of stones spreads in a solid mass more than 100 feet in breadth though sometimes narrowed to 80 and 50 feet. But out and beyond the solid sheet of *debris*, the stones in less close array have gone down the steep descent to the very base of the mountain. Supposing all these stones to be restored to their original places on the great bulwark, we must conclude that its height had been very great, and in some just proportion to its singular breadth.

Near the middle of the terrace above mentioned, there is a gap in the great wall, which was likely the chief entrance to the fort. A street of the remains of round houses lines the whole course of the wall which defends this terrace.

These round houses, which vary in size, are a remarkable feature in this fortress. Some of them are oval, and, as a rule, they seem to be designed to fill up the whole space between the great bulwark and the slope of the hill. But a portion of the terrace is broader than they could fully occupy, and there appears to have been an inner fort wall, as it were behind them. The surrounding wall of all these round houses appears to be 10 feet broad, and where it comes between two houses it becomes what is now called a mutual wall. This seems to have been the arrangement along the whole range, the only exception being the wall of the circle farthest south, which is the largest on the hill.

It is to be observed that, though each of this long line of round houses presses close upon the great fort wall—so close that no space remains between them—yet they are perfectly distinct buildings, and their masonry has no connection with the masonry of the walls. Each house has its unbroken circle, and the fort wall has its unbroken line of regularly-laid masonry. Unlike as this method is to our own practice in building, it was a most judicious one in their circumstances.

The most southern member of this long range or street of round houses is the largest of the number, its diameter within the walls being more than 30 feet. Its walls also seem to have been broader than those of the others, and have been built of stones of far greater dimensions, which appear to have stood on end in " Druid circle " fashion. Close beside this round house there is a well-built descending spiral stair, probably that of a well. On the north-west side of the hill there are the remains of an entrance way into the fort. The wall may be traced running up in a straight line through a vast mass of ruins, and may have reached from the inner to the second wall. Along its line there are such a number of unusually large stones that one would be inclined to think they had formed the roof of the gallery, of which this wall was a part. Miss Maclagan opened up some 40 feet of this line of

E

wall, and felt a strong desire for further investigation, but found it to be rather dangerous work, the steepness of the ascent causing the loosened stones to descend upon the excavators.

On the south and east front of the hill, and nearer the summit than the outer wall by 60 feet, there is another wall extending 209 feet in length, within which are the remains of two circular houses. It is difficult to determine the original breadth of this wall, but the amount of *debris* on the slope beneath it seems to indicate that it was both broad and high. It is quite possible that there were other walls belonging to this fort ; indeed there are indications of such, but somewhat too faint to be relied upon.

Viewed even in its present ruinous condition, the Mither Tap is the most notable of all our ancient forts. Outside the chief wall of the fort, to the north of the main entrance, there is a rock-platform of a triangular shape. This also has been fortified by a wall built of far larger stones than any of the others, some of these stones being not less than 10 feet in length. This wall is greatly destroyed, the wasting of the rock on which it rested having caused its downfall. Evidently the military authorities who built the fort had observed that this platform of rock was too near their fortress to be left at the discretion of an enemy, and though quite outside their own circumvallations they thought it well to keep possession of it.

GARBIT AND BRUNTWOOD TAPS.

These tops are to the south-west of the Mither Tap, and are worth a passing glance only. They are small crags, of little interest except when viewed from the

Don, from which they have a striking enough appearance. Below the former is Quarry Hill, called also the "English Quarry," because it was worked by an English Company, the granite blocks being sent to Sheerness for dock-building purposes. It is upwards of seventy years ago since the quarry ceased to be worked. Below it may be seen the ruins of a building which was used as the quarry "smiddy." Some forty years ago a "character," Jamieson, took possession of the ruined smiddy and lived in it, as mentioned in a later chapter, for several years. Garbit Tap is about 1540 feet, and Bruntwood Tap about 1350 feet, in height. There is a spring between them—the whole mountain, as has been seen, being well supplied with water. Above Garbit Tap is a rude open shelter, and on the rocky top is the inscription

indicating the portions of Bennachie which fell to the two estates Logie-Elphinstone and Tillyfour on the division of the Commonty. The former's share is to the north, the latter's to the south, of Garbit Tap.

MILLSTONE HILL.

Millstone (familiarly Millstane) Hill claims to be *a spur*, not *a top*, of Bennachie. It is separated from its parent by Clachie Burn running eastward and Birks Burn running in a westerly direction, the former between it and the Mither Tap. Near the source of Birks Burn are the ruins of "Birks" farm-steading.

But the farm has passed out of cultivation, its height—700 to 800 feet—and situation rendering the production and ingathering of crops sometimes uncertain and unprofitable ; but perhaps also " game" may have had something to do with the clearance. The hill is wooded and heathery to the top, and has no distinctive feature, the summit being flattish, with a small cairn. It owes its name, as stated in the first chapter, to the fact of millstones having been quarried on it.

CHAPTER IV.

ITS BALLAD LORE.

THE GIANT OF THE HILL.

According to tradition, Bennachie was of old guarded by a giant, known by the name of Jock o' Bennachie. Jock's dimensions were somewhat enormous, as may be understood from the extent of ground which he required for his bed. The bed is still shown, and is known as " Little John's Length," Jock, despite his exceptional height, being familiarly styled " Little Johnnie." Little John's Length, as already stated, is situated to the east of Craig Shannoch, and is the space between two small craigs, the lower of which has been recently quarried. One of these craigs is about 1440 feet, and the other 1400, above sea level. The distance between them is about 600 feet, so that Jock must have been tall, even for a giant. The spot where Jock dried his " sark " is also pointed out on the north-west of Craig Shannoch, and is easily distinguishable as the ascent is made from Oyne. It has a general resemblance to the garment named, being produced by the heather and turf having been at one time cut away from a bit of the hill face.

Jock seems to have required all his huge proportions to combat with his foes, who were both powerful and numerous, his principal opponent being Jock o' Noth. Noth is a well-known hill in the parish of Rhynie and district of Strathbogie, some

thirteen miles to the north-west of Bennachie.
That distance did not prevent a pretty frequent
exchange of compliments, in the shape of huge
boulders, between the two. On Tap o' Noth (it is
said !) may yet be seen a stone with the mark of five
gigantic fingers thereon, which, according to popular
tradition, was thrown by Jock o' Bennachie from Oxen
Craig at Jock o' Noth. The latter, on this particular
occasion, retaliated by raising a huge mass of rock
with the view of hurling it to the mountain of the
Garioch, when Jock o' Bennachie put out his foot, just
touching the mass. The result was that it never left
Tap o' Noth, and, indeed, if you care to look, you
will find the mark of Jock's toe thereon !

Jock has been accused of throwing stones at the
priest of Kemnay—a man of great piety, as Mr.
Cadenhead's ballad, given at the end of this chapter,
tells. But of course this is a mistake ! Besides,
Jock, like most other big men, was of a peaceful, not
to say kindly, nature. He, while he succeeded in
defending himself against his visible foes, had ultimately to succumb to enchantment, and is buried in a
cave, somewhere on the mountain that he was wont to
guard. But let it be understood Jock is not dead—
he is merely under a spell, secured by lock and key.
Of course the key is lost, but as one version of a
prophecy already quoted, says :

> A wife's ae sin wi' ae e'e
> Sall fin' the kyey o' Bennachie,

and then the giant will be freed. The prophecy remains unfulfilled, however : the key has not yet been
found, and poor Jock lies spell-bound in his unknown
cave on Bennachie, where once he ruled supreme.

The two ballads that follow, the Rival Giants and the
Key o' Bennachie, tell of Jock and his fate :

THE RIVAL GIANTS.

For lang the earth wi' drought was tried,
　The sun shone down fierce rays ;
At length heaven's flood-gates were let loose—
　It rained for twenty days.

Now, bonnie shone the sun upon
　The Hill o' Bennachie ;
And ilka blade o' grass it had
　A tear drap in its e'e.

The birds were singin' i' the lift
　A gladsome, joyous strain,
And ilka livin' thing agreed
　To sing in praise o' rain.

A' livin' thing, exceptin' ane,
　Looked up to heaven and sang ;
But Jock, the keeper o' the hill,
　To praise he wadna gang.

For " slichted love is sair to bide,"
　And Jock was very loth
To gie his love, his Lady Anne,
　As wife to Jock o' Noth.

" Oh, Lady Anne ! oh, Lady Anne !
　Ye reck nae what ye do,
To tempt me thus, when ye ken well
　I love but only you."

Then up he raise frae aff his bed,
　And shook himsel' richt free !
" Now by my saul, I'se let him ken
　I'm Jock o' Bennachie. "

He's taen a stane, his pillow 'twas,
　He's gripped it hard and ticht,
" Now by my troth, to Tap o' Noth
　The stane I'll throw this nicht. "

E'en as he spak his rival stood
    Upon his ain hill-tap ;
A buirdly chiel, wi' fearless mien,
    Nae dreadin' a mishap.

Beside him stood the Lady Anne,
    The love-licht in her e'e ;
She thochtna, as he kissed her lips,
    They were sae soon to dee.

Wi' steady hand Jock took his aim,
    He swore a fearfu' aith,
Syne thro' the air he flung the stane,
    And killed the lovers baith.

.   .   .   .

The stane still lies upon the hill,
    Its weicht nae man can tell,
For ever since that fatal day
    It's lain where it fell.

Now, ye that are incredulous,
    Just gang to Bennachie,
And on the stane on Tap o' Noth
    Jock's finger-marks ye'll see.

.   .   .   .

Oh, bonnie shone the sun upon
    The Hill o' Bennachie,
And ilka blade o' grass it had
    A tear-drap in its e'e.

The birds were singing i' the lift
    A joyous, gladsome strain,
And ilka livin' thing agreed
    To sing in praise o' rain.

THE KEY O' BENNACHIE.

Upon the hill o' Bennachie
    There lived lang years agane
A gaint loon, an', Samson-like,
    He feared neen—gods nor men.

His bed was 'tween twa little craigs,
    Sax hunner feet apairt ;
An' there he lay the lee-lang day,
    A lazy, easy mairt.

His bleach-green was the braid hillside,
    An' there his sark he dried ;
A wife to wash't he couldna get,
    Tho' he had aften tried.

Sae in the Gadie he wad sweel't,
    An' wring't wi' baith his han's,
Syne spread it oot upo' the hill
    In carefu' nine-inch spans.

But life was unco dreich an' drear
    To Jock o' Bennachie,
An' aft he'd lie an' sich an' sigh,
    "Oh, wha'll be wife to me?"

.   .   .   .

The nicht was eerie, cauld, an' mirk,
    An', in his "little bed,"
Jock slept—when lo ! soft music swept
    In sweet strains o'er his head.

Then swiftly, swiftly raise he up,
    An', rubbin' baith his een,
He lookit at a vision rare,
    The rarest he had seen.

A lady fair, wi' gowden hair
    (But, oh, her face was wan),
Sic witchin' grace, an' winnin' air—
    "Can ye be Lady Anne?"

She look'd sae wistfu' in his een,
    That, thinkin't nae amiss,
He raised her up, an' on her lips
    He fondly pressed a kiss.

But a' was dark where licht had been,
    A maist unearthly licht ;
An' doon they sank, doon thro' the hill
    They baith gaed, oot o' sicht.

Then to the thunder's weirdly roar,
    The lichtnin's flashin' streak,
The hinges o' an unseen door
    Were heard to groan an' creak.

An' bolts were shot, a key was turned ;
    The heavens ceased their war.
Still as the grave was a' thing, save
    The cock's crow from afar.

    .   .   .   .   .   .

An' never sin' that awfu' nicht
    Has Jock by mortal e'e
Been seen, or heard o' far or near,
    Nor ever has the key

Been found—the key that locked them in,
    Some think it's i' the sea,
An' Jock o' Bennachie's been left
    Inside the hill to dee !

But whether he be deid or no,
    " An' ae sin wi' ae e'e,"
'Tis sagely said, " sall," some day, " fin'"
    The Key o' Bennachie."

From the Giant of the Hill we pass on to

LANG JOHNNIE MOIR.

The local ballad, " Lang Johnnie Moir," in spite of
its great length, is very interesting, if only as a sample
of the old localised narrative ballad.   It shows that the
two giants of Bennachie and Tap o' Noth could, when
occasion demanded, cease fighting with each other
and combine their forces.   The ballad is undoubtedly
very old, but when composed is a matter very difficult
to determine.   Some years ago I got it taken down in
writing from an old friend in the parish of Oyne, since
deceased, who was very fond of occasionally going

over a few verses of it to those who cared for such things. The ballad has long been a great favourite at the foot of Bennachie, though, at the time I speak of, it was not known locally to have been in type. The present version differs a good deal from that in Peter Buchan's "Ancient Ballads and Songs of the North of Scotland" (1828, reprinted in 1875), besides being longer, but I believe it will be found to agree best with the local rendering. As I received it, several of the verses were transposed, and there was otherwise some little difficulty at times in following the story, but without violence having been done, the ballad is now presented as nearly perfect in form and order as may be. Tradition says that the hero lived in the neighbourhood of Harthill Castle ; beyond that notes are superfluous —the story speaks for itself :

LANG JOHNNIE MOIR.

There lived a lad in Garioch's land,
    An' anither in Auchindoir,
But the bonniest lad among them a'
    Was Lang Johnnie Moir.

> *Chorus*—A riddle ow, leel dum daddie,
>   A riddle, a leel dum dee.

Johnnie he was weel brought up,
    Baith sturdy, stoot, an' strang,
An' the blade that hung by Johnnie's side
    Was fully ten feet lang.

Johnnie was a clever youth,
    Fu' sturdy, stoot, an' wight ;
He was three yards around the waist,
    An' fourteen feet in hight.

Johnnie he is on to fair London,
    If a' be true we hear ;
Johnnie's on to fair London,
    The king's banner to bear.

He hadna been in fair London
   Months but barely three,
When the fairest lady in a' the land
   Fell in love wi' young Johnnie.

Word's gaein up and word's gaein doon,
   Till it cam tae the King,
That the muckle Scot had fa'en in love
   Wi' his dother Lady Jean.

"If this be true," the King he said,
   "That ye dae tell to me,
That weighty Scot sall stretch a rope—
   High hanged sall he be."

When Johnnie heard his sentence passed
   A licht, licht lauch gaed he,
An', as he clapped his trusty blade,
   "Ye darena a' hang me."

But the English rogues are cunning dogs—
   Aboot him they did creep,
An' gaed him draps o' lodomy
   That lulled him fast asleep.

When Johnnie waukened oot o's sleep
   A sorry man was he—
His hands in bars of iron bands,
   His feet in fetters three.

"A curse upon their lodomy,
   It bore me such a sway ;
Three o' their men—the bravest three—
   They bore my blade away.

"Faur will I fin' a bonnie boy
   That'll work for meat an' fee,
That will rin on to my uncle,
   To the fit o' Bennachie?"

"Here am I, a bonnie boy,
   That'll work for meat an' fee,
That'll rin on to fair Scotland,
   To the fit o' Bennachie."

" When ye come to whaur water's strong
   Ye'll bend yir bow and swim ;
When ye come to whaur grass grows green
   Ye'll slack yir shune an' rin.

" And when ye come to Bennachie
   Ye'll neither chap nor ca',
But well ye'll ken aul' Johnnie there,
   Three feet abune them a'.

" Ye'll gie him this braid letter,
   Sealed wi' my faith and troth,
And ye'll bid him bring alang wi' him
   The buirdly Jock o' Noth."

And when he came to waters strong
   He bent his bow and swam ;
And when he came whaur grass grew green
   He slack'd his shune an' ran.

And when he came to Bennachie
   He did neither chap nor ca',
For weel he kent aul' Johnnie there,
   Three feet abune them a'.

" What news, what news, my little boy ?
   Ye was never here before."
" Nae news, nae news, but a letter, sir,
   Fae your nephew, Johnnie Moir.

" Here is a letter fae his hand,
   Sealed wi' his faith an' troth,
And ye're bidden bring alang wi' you
   The buirdly Jock o' Noth."

Bennachie lies very low,
   And Tap o' Noth lies high ;
But for a' the miles them atween,
   Jock heard aul' Johnnie cry.

Swift ran these men o'er hills an' dales,
   An' swiftly o'er the lea,
And they did reach fair London
   By dawning the third day.

An' whan they cam' to fair London
　　The yetts were a' shut in,
The drums did beat, an' the trumpets sound,
　　An' they made a doleful din.

An' whan they cam' to fair London
　　The yetts were lock't wi' bands ;
An' wha wis there but a trumpeter
　　Wi's trumpet in his hands.

" Fat's the maitter, ye keepers a',
　　An' fat's adee within,
That drums do beat and bells do ring,
　　An' mak sic doleful din ? "

" There's naething adee," the keeper said,
　　" There's naething adee for thee,
But a michtie Scot to stretch a rope ;
　　Neist mornin' he maun dee."

" Open your yetts," says Jock o' Noth,
　　" It's open them to me ; "
The English keeper trembling said,
　　" Sir, I've not got the key.

" Open your yetts," says Jock o' Noth,
　　" It's open them to me,
For there's a body at my back
　　Fae Scotland brocht the key."

" Open your yetts," says Jock o' Noth,
　　" It's open at my ca' ; "
Wi' that he knock'd doon wi' his fit
　　Three ells' breadth o' their wa'.

As they gaed in by Drury Lane,
　　An' doon by the Toon Ha',
'Twas there they saw young Johnnie Moir
　　Stan' on their English wa'.

" Ye're welcome here, my uncle dear,
　　Thrice welcome unto me,
Ye'll loose this knot, an' slack this rope,
　　An' take me fae the tree."

" Is it for murder or for theft,
  Or is't for robberie?
If 'tis for ony heinous crime
  There's nae remeid for thee."

" It's neither for murder, nor yet for theft,
  Nor yet for robberie;
But it's a' for lovin' a lady fair,
  An' for her I maun dee."

" Oh, whaur's yer soord," says Jock o' Noth,
  " Ye brocht fae Scotland wi' thee?
I never kent a Scotchman yet
  But could wield a soord or tree."

" A curse upon their lodomy,
  On me it'd sic a sway;
Three o' their men, the bravest three,
  Did tak' my blade away."

" Bring back his soord," says Jock o' Noth,
  " An' gie't to him fu' free,
Or I hae sworn a big Scotch aith
  I'll gar ten thoosan' dee."

" Noo, whaur's the lady," says Jock o' Noth,
  " For fain I would her see?"
" She's lockit up in her ain room,
  The King he keeps the key."

Sae they hae gane afore the King,
  Wi' courage bold an' free;
Their armour bricht cast sic a licht,
  It almost dimm'd his e'e.

An' whan they cam' afore the King,
  Twa ghastly guests were they;
Between their eyes there was a yaird,
  Between their shoo'ders three.

"Oh, whaur's the lady," says Jock o' Noth,
  " For fain I would her see?
We're baith come to her weddin',
  Fae the fit o' Bennachie.

"Sae bring yer dother doon, oh King,
    That we her weel may see ;
For we hae sworn a big Scotch aith
    She'll gang to Bennachie."

"Tak 'er an' welcome," said the King,
    " For ye welcome are for me ;
I never thocht there were sic men
    At the fit o' Bennachie."

The Sheriff an' the guard likewise
    Stood a' amazed to see
The little body Jock o' Noth,
    An' Jock o' Bennachie.

"If I had kent " said Jock o' Noth,
    " Ye'd wunn'ert sae much at me,
I would hae brocht a biggar man
    For size as three times three ;
It's Arthur Spark, baith stout and stark,
    He's fifty feet an' three."

" Accursed be the bonnie boy
    That brocht the tidin's to thee ;
Lat England say whate'er it may,
    High hanged sall he be."

" If ye dae hang the bonnie boy
    That brocht the tidin's tae me,
I will come to his burial—
    Rewarded shall he be."

"Tak 'er, an' welcome," said the King —
    " Lat me never hear o' thee ;
Tak'er an' welcome," said the King,
    " An' the boy he sall go free."
" A priest, a priest," then Johnnie cried,
    " Tae join my love an' me."

" A clerk, a clerk," the King replied,
    " Tae seal her tocher wi' thee."
But noo oot speaks aul' Johnnie Moir,
    These words lat fa' did he—

" I wintna lands nor rents at hame,
    Sae keep yer gowd for me ;
An' I've plenishin' an' plenty,
    An' thirty ploughs an' three ;
An' I fa' heir to ane estate
    At the fit o' Bennachie.

" Hae ye ony masons in yer toon,
    Or ony at yer ca',
That ye may noo them quickly send
    An' big yer broken wa'?"

" Oh, I hae masons in my toon,
    There's plenty at my ca' ;
But gang yer wauys to whaur ye cam',
    Nor min' the broken wa'."

They've ta'en the lady by the han',
    Set her frae prison free—
The drums did beat, the pipes did play,
    An' the nicht was spent in glee.

Noo aul' Johnnie Moir, an' young Johnnie Moir,
    An' Jock o' Noth—a' three—
An' the London lady, an' the bonnie boy,
    Went a' to Bennachie.

An' if a' be true that ilk ane says,
    As a' is true we see,
Young Johnnie an' she live happy lives
    At the fit o' Bennachie.

THE WEE, WEE MAN O' BENNACHIE.

The following are the first and last verses of a ballad,
entitled "The Little Man," which is to be found in
Buchan's Ballads:

As I gaed oot to tak' the air,
    Between Midmar and bonny Craigha',
There I met a little wee man,
    The less o' him I never saw.

*   *   *   *   *

F

Oot gat the lichts, on cam' the mist,
  Ladies nor mannie mair cou'd see ;
I turned about, an' gae a look,
  Just at the fit o' Bennachie.

This ballad, which should be read in conjunction with
"The Wee, Wee Man" of *Scottish Ballads*, published
by Blackie & Son, 1845, has been rendered in another
shape, under the title of "The Wee, Wee Man o' Bennachie":

THE WEE, WEE MAN O' BENNACHIE.

As I strayed me down by the windin' Don,
  Bright was the nicht—the moon shone clear,
The grass, laich whisp'rin' to the breeze,
  Wi' the flutter o' leaves, was a' I could hear.

'Twas atween Midmar and bonny Craigha'
  That I spied wi' my een richt rarely
A wee, wee mannie sae trig an' sae blythe,
  An' oh but he spak me sae fairly.

He was but a wee bit hop-o'-my-thumb,
  But a leg baith strong and supple I ween ;
His teeth gleamed oot sae bonny and white,
  Did this wee mannie's that I hae seen.

Atween his brows there was but a span,
  Frae shouther to shouther in ells count three,
But he lifted a stane, 'twas sax feet high,
  An' he laid it langways ower his knee.

His leg he swang't baith back an' fore
  Aucht times, as I micht fairly count it,
An' guid fifty yards an' mair, I trow,
  The stane thro' the air he swiftly shountet.

"Now, be ye an elf, or be ye the deil,
  I fain wi' you to your dwallin' would hie."
Oh, sauftly he leuch, an' faintly he sighed,
  "My bower, fair lady, is nae very nigh.

" Your wish is a law, an' if ye'll but come,
    Richt proudly I'll shaw ye my castle gay ;
Gin ye but loup on o' my coal black steed,
    Oh ! we will be there gin screich o' day."

Sae on we lap an' away we rade,
    His arm gaed roun my middle sae sma',
An' he's ta'en a kiss frae my red lips,
    Afore we hae sichtet fair Craigha'.

Oh, by Balquhain gaed we, an' by Harthill
    We flew as tho' his horse had wings ;
He has vowed to be mine, my ain true love,
    Just as the curfew slowly rings.

We rade till we cam' to the castle wa',
    " What ho ! there, keeper, lat down the brig !"
An' in we rade thro' the big, big yett ;
    I trow, but the wa's were bonny an' trig.

The kipples were made o' the guid red gowd,
    An' the reef it was o' the proseyla' ;
The tapestries rare an' the curtains hung
    Round ilka bit o' the castle ha'.

The ha' it was full o' dancers gay,
    The ladies wi' waists baith jimp an' sma',
But at ilka turn o' the weird-like dance,
    The wee, wee mannie was wearin' awa'.

Then oot gaed the lichts, an' the mist cam' down,
    But dancers nor man nae mair could I see ;
I turned me roun', an' rubbit my een,
    An' found myself sittin' on Bennachie.

As I strayed me down by the windin' Don,
    The moon shone bricht, an' clear was the air,
The grass an' the leaves baith spak' to the breeze ;
    A' nature was busily whisperin' there.

THE BONNIE LASS O' BENNACHIE.

The following ballad has long been a great favourite
in the Garioch and at the "foot o' Bennachie":

THE BONNIE LASS O' BENNACHIE.

Once I loved a lady fair,
She was a beauty, I declare,
The loveliest flower in the north countrie,
The Bonnie Lass o' Bennachie.

She being an heiress of house and land,
And I alone a poor farmer's son,
It was her birth and high degree
That parted my true love and me.

I loved this lady in my heart,
Against our wills it was to part,
For she adored me as her life ;
In private we were man and wife.

Great knights and squires a-courting came
To see this fair and lovely dame,
But all their offers proved in vain,
For none her favour could obtain.

But when her father came to know
How that I loved his daughter so,
He, Judas-like, betrayed me,
For the keeping of her company.

'Twas at Old Rayne where I was ta'en
A prisoner for Lady Jean,
In fetters strong there I was bound,
And carried on to Aberdeen.

But it's not their frowns, love, that I do mind,
Nor yet the way that I have to go,
But love has pierced my tender heart,
And alas ! it's brought me very low.

I was embarked at the shore—
My native land to see no more—
In Germany a soldier to be,
All for the lass o' Bennachie.

But when I was upon the seas,
I ne'er could get a moment's ease :
For she was daily in my mind,
The bonnie lass I left behind.

When I arrived in Germany,
From my true love a letter came
With her respects in each degree,
Signed by the lass o' Bennachie.

The answer which to her I sent,
It never to my true love went ;
Her cruel father told her then
That I abroad was surely slain,

Which grieved this maiden's heart full sore,
To think that we should meet no more ;
It caused her weep most bitterly,
Those tidings from high Germany.

" Oh, daughter dear, from tears refrain,
To weep for him it is in vain—
I have a better match for thee,
To enjoy the lands o' Bennachie."

" But he was the husband of my youth.
In pledge he had my faith and troth ;
I've made a vow I'll wed with none,
Since my true love is dead and gone."

On every finger she put a ring,
On her mid finger she put three ;
And she's away to high Germany
In hopes her true love yet to see.

She was dressed in robes of green,
Which was most comely to be seen.
Oh ! had he been a crownéd king
This lady fair might his have been.

When she arrived in Germany,
By fortune there her true love did see
Upon a lofty rampart wall
As he was standing sentry.

" Oh, were my true love in this country,
It's I would say that you were she,
For there's not a face so full of grace,
Not in all the lands of Germany."

The first she met was Colonel Shand,
And he addressed her courteously,
From where she came and where was bound,
Her home, and of what country.

"From fair Scotland," she says, "I come
In hopes my true love for to see,
For I am told he is a Grenadier
Into your lordship's company."

"What's thy love's name, my comely dame?
Oh, lady fair, do tell to me;
In the station of a single man,
It's a sair pity that he should be."

"Oh, William Graham is my love's name,
All these hardships he suffers for me:
But though it should cost me thousands ten,
A single man no more he'll be."

Young Billy Graham was called then
His own love once more to see,
But when he saw her well-faured face,
Oh, the salt tears did blind his e'e.

"You're welcome here, my dearest love,
You are thrice welcome here to me,
For there's not a face so full of grace,
Not in all the lands o' Germany."

But when her father came to know
That his daughter abroad had gone,
He sent a letter, on express it was,
To call these two lovers home.

With kisses sweet these lovers met
Most joyfully, as I am told;
She's changed his dress from worsted lace
To crimson and scarlet trimmed with gold.

To him he gave a full discharge,
All for the sake of Lady Jean,
And now, I am told, he's a wealthy squire
Into the shire of Aberdeen.

But now behold how fortune turns
Her father's rage to vanity,
For now he lives in sweet content
With his Bonnie Lass o' Bennachie.

HOSIE'S WELL.

Hosie's Well has already been referred to, and
the following legendary account of it, by Mr. Arthur
King, will doubtless be found interesting.

HOSIE'S WELL.

A LEGEND OF BENNACHIE.

Oh, ken ye Hosie's Well that springs
    Frae oot a mossy gap,
As ye gang up tae Bennachie,
    Close by the Mither Tap?

The water bubbles pure an' fresh,
    An' caller is beside ;
An', oh, but Hosie's Well's weel kent
    In a' the kintra side.

Fan feudal fechts war common things,
    An' reivin' wis an airt,
There dwalt a man by Bennachie
    Fa head an honest hert.

Wi' honest hert he lo'ed a maid,
    An' lo'ed by her wis he ;
Nae truer herts than theirs wis kent
    A' roon by Bennachie.

For Hosie wis an honest chiel,
    An' a gallant lad forbye ;
An' he had walth o' warl's gear,
    An' fifty heid o' kye !

Foo aften did they wander roon
    The hill, fan wark wis deen,
Their herts baith speakin' words o' love,
    An' love looks in their cen.

Sae Hosie's taen a ring o' gowd
    An' pitten't in her han';
He swore that he wad share wi' Jean
    His gowd, his gear, an' lan'.

"It's I sall be yer ain gudeman,
    An' ye sall be my wife;
An' I'll lat naething e'er come ower
    My Jean through a' her life.

"It's I will tak' ye tae my hert,
    Faur ye sall dwall always;
An' a' yer life sall summer be,
    An' brichter than sun's rays."

An' sae he's ta'en her till his hert,
    An' kissed her three times three,
While the laverock sang a joyous note
    On the side o' Bennachie.

"It's I will be yer true love, John,
    It's I'll be ever true;
An' naething in this warl' sall tak'
    My love awa' frae you."

An' sae the time flew quickly on
    Till Hosie's weddin' day
Cam' roon, an' a' the kintra side
    Wis there in gran' array.

An' Jean wis deckit in her braws,
    An' wore her kirtle green,
St. Ninian's Priest haed scarce begood
    Tae mak' them baith as ane,

Fan up there rose an' awfu' cry,
    That roon wis heard for miles —
"Up, up, brave lads; defen' yersel's
    Frae Donald o' the Isles !"

Then ilka ane flew oot the hoose,
    His broadsword in his han',
An' rushed awa' tae deal a blow
    Tae Donald's reivin' ban'.

The Priest o' Ninian's boo't his heid,
   An' cross'd himsel' an' said,
"We'd better a' look tae oorsells,"
   Then hade below the bed !

Sae Hosie's taen his gweed claymore,
   An' kissed his blushin' bride,
An', jumpin' on his milk-white horse,
   Awa' tae Harlaw hied !

An' bonnie Jean, nae yet a wife,
   Wi' saut tears tricklin' doun,
There prayt that Hosie might be brocht
   Back tae her safe an' soun'.

Fan Hosie got tae reed Harlaw,
   He focht wi' micht an' main ;
An' on the Hielan' heids his blows
   Fell fast as winter's rain.

Fan Donald's men wis beaten back,
   He chased them wi' a will,
Until he wis ta'en prisoner
   By Donald on the hill.

They took him tae the far-aff Isles,
   Faur stood the chieftain's Keep,
An' keepit him for three lang years,
   Chyned in a dungeon deep.

An' bonnie Jean, baith nicht an' day,
   For Hosie aye murn't sair,
Till ae day cam' a gallant by,
   An' Jean, she sigh'd nae mair !

The gallant's speech wis fair an' fine,
   His claes war unco braw,
An' Jean's hert gaed the bigger loups
   The mair o' him she saw.

They wandered aft by Bennachie,
   Aye did they, weel-a-wat !
She listened tae his love faur she
   An' Hosie aft haed sat.

He took a ring frae aff his han',
    An' pit it upo' hers ;
The win' sough'd wi' an eerie soun'
    Amang the tossin' firs.

Ae nicht Jean an' her gallant Sir
    Gaed up tae Bennachie ;
They spied a man wi' towzy hair
    An' madness in his e'e.

There on that bank faur Jean had pledged
    Tae Hosie tae be true,
Sat Hosie waitin' for his love,
    An' him richt weel she knew !

" Ah, gentle lady an' guid sir,
    I pray ye tell tae me
If there is ane ca'd Bonnie Jean
    Bides noo near Bennachie ?

" For she lo'ed me an' I lo'ed her,
    Aye lo'ed her weel did I ;
An' gin she lives she'll lo'e me noo,
    As in the days gane bye.

" Oh, curses on the bluidy han'
    That reeve my love frae me ;
Bit I've come back tae keep my tryste,
    Here on auld Bennachie !

" Oh, ye wha seem true lovers noo,
    Jist listen till I tell
The story o' an honest love,
    An' fat that love befell !

" 'Twas on the day o' reed Harlaw,
    I stood wi' a' my pride
Wi' Jean afore St. Ninian's Priest—
    My Jean, my bonnie bride.

" I jist had ta'en her han' in mine,
    Tae pairt for never mair,
Fan Donald o' the Isles cam' doon
    Tae lay the kintra bare !

" I had tae leave my Jean afore
 We were made man an' wife,
Tae deal a blow against the foe
 In Harlaw's bluidy strife !

' I focht the fecht, an' chased the foe
 Up wast for mony miles,
Fan I a prisoner wis ta'en
 By Donald o' the Isles.

" For weary three years I hae lain
 In a Keep close by the sea,
Bit fat car't I, sae lang's I kent
 My Jean wis true tae me !

" Ae day I loupit o'er the wa's,
 An' focht the crested faem,
An' struggled wi' o'erpow'ring foes
 That I micht jist get hame.

" 'Twas here Jean said she lo'ed but me,
 Aye, here jist gane three year ;
An' noo I'll wyte until she comes,
 It's I will wyte her here !

" It's I s'all sit an' wyte her here
 Tho't sud be a' my life ;
An' syne we'll tae her faither's hoose,
 An' come out man an' wife !

" I've cried upon the hills an' crags,
 I've cried upon ilk tree,
That giff my ain true love's alive
 That she will come tae me !

" But giff my ain true love be deid
 She'll come a' dress't sae bricht ;
But somethieg tells my hert she's near—
 She's near tae me the nicht !

" For mony days I've sat an' grat,
 An' for as mony years
I'll sit an' weep for my lost love,
 Until my Jean appears—

" Until my love comes back tae me,
    An' tells me she's been true,
An' syne we'll be as happy, sir,
    As your sweet maid an' you ! "

Syne Jean fell deed upon the grun',
    An' Hosie breathed his last ;
The owlets croaked an eerie note,
    An' fiercer shrieked the blast.

They buriet Jean deep i' the mools
    'Side Bennachie sae sweet,
An' Hosie he wis laid at rest
    Jist on the spot he deet.

They buriet him deep i' the grun',
    An' there he lies aleen,
Aye there he weeps frae morn till nicht
    Awaitin' for his Jean.

Four hunner an' auchty years hae gane—
    At least that's what they tell—
But the tears o' Hosie yet spring up
    At the place ca'd " Hosie's Well."

For it's richt weel kent in a' the lan',
    An' his been kent for years,
That the water that rises in Hosie's Well
    Is naething but Hosie's tears !

THE DEVIL'S STANE O' KEMNAY.

Mr. William Cadenhead's ballad on the Devil's
Stone, referred to in Chapter II., under the heading
"From Kemnay," is most interesting, and shows an
intimate knowledge of the district.   It is entitled

THE DEVIL'S STANE O' KEMNAY.

Oh, meek was the soul o' the monk that prayed
    At Logie Durno's shrine ;
And Braco's priest was fired with zeal
    When he touched on theme divine.

And there was a stream o' fervour deep,
    And a fund o' godly lear,
For ever pourand frae the lips
    O' the Friar o' Fetternear.

And they were haly men and guid,
    The chanons o' Monymusk,
For they prayed the souls o' the quick and the dead
    Frae dawning day till dusk.

But Logie Durno, Monymusk,
    Or Braco, or Fetternear,
Could ne'er, for kindliness o' heart,
    Wi' the priest o' Kemnay peer.

For Braco might pray for Schir Andro's soul,
    Whose red blood did atone
For harrying Inneravin's lands,
    And stealing the " Maid o' Stradone."

And the guid Culdees o' Monymusk
    Might plead for King Malcolm's repose,
Wha vow'd to Sanct Andrew, their haly house,
    For victory o'er his foes.

But oh ! for lifting the downcast heart—
    For helping the lowly poor—
For pourring ane balm on the troubled soul
    And soothing life's parting hour—

On a' the bonnie banks o' Don
    There wasna ane haly man
Like him wha knelt at Kemnay Kirk,
    At the shrine o' our Lady Anne.

The fiend wha dwells in the bottomless pit,
    ' Mang byrnand flame and stour,
And roams the yearth like ane roarand lion
    For wham he may devour,

Aft cast his e'e on Kemnay's priest,
    Wi' ane fierce and vilefu' look—
For beand the fae o' human kind,
    It's frien's he canna bruik.

And aft when he stoppit his vengefu' flight
  On the tap o' Bennachie,
He vowed and swore that the haly priest
  A bitter death sud die !

For far, far back in the aulden time,
  ' Tis said that Bennachie
Was ane o' the ports o' the byrnand pit,
  Whaur the wicked torment dree ;

That it flared wi' fire i' the midnight sky,
  And spew'd out smoke at noon,
Till its very stonen foundiments
  Frae its tap ran myltand doon.

And the fiend aft sat on his auld door-stane,
  Plotting an evil deed,
And aye the tither curse was hurled
  At the priest o' Kemnay's head !

It was the feast o' Sanct Barnabas,
  I' the merry month o' June,
When the woods are a' in their green livery,
  And the wild birds a' in tune ;

And the priest o' Kemnay has gane to the kirk,
  And prayed an earnest prayer—
" That Sathan might for ever be bound
  To his dark and byrnand lair ! "

And aye the haly organ rung,
  And the sound rose higher—higher,
Till they reached the fiend on Bennachie,
  And he bit his nails for ire.

And he lookit east, and he lookit west,
  And he lookit aboon—beneath ;
But nocht could he see, save the bauld grey rocks,
  That glower'd out through the heath.

He lifted aloft a ponderous rock,
  And hurl'd it through the air—
" Twere pity ye sud want reward
  For sae devout a prayer ! "

The Miller o' Kemany cries to his knave,
    " Lift up the back sluice, loon !
For a cloud comes o'er frae Bennachie
    Enough the mill to droon."

The boatman hurries his boat ashore,
    And fears he'll be ower late—
" Giff yon black cloud comes doon in rain
    It's fit to raise a spate !"

But the ponderous rock came on and on,
    Well aimed for Kemnay Kirk,
And cross'd it field, or cross'd it flood,
    Its shadow gar'd a' grow mirk.

But the fervent prayers o' the haly priest,
    And the power o' the sweet Sanct Anne,
They turned the murderous rock aside,
    And foiled the foul fiend's plan.

And it lichted doon frae the darkened lift,
    Like the greedy erne bird,
And there it sits in the Kirk-lands yet,
    Half buried in the yird.

CHAPTER V.

THE COMMONTY.

Bennachie was, till 1859, a commonty, being frequently spoken of as the Free or King's Forest of Bennachie. The Rev. Dr. George Skene Keith, in his "Agriculture of Aberdeenshire" (1811), says it was "formerly a royal forest," and in the "View of the Diocese of Aberdeen" it is stated: "This was one of the King's forests of old, and is full of moss still, and begins now to be planted with firs. It now affords pasture to the sheep of the neighbouring gentry, but is greatly infested with foxes. Here is a rock which affords a sort of coarse diamond of the black kind " [referring probably to a dark variety of quartz crystals frequently found in the red granite of the hill]. It is, however, by no means certain that it was, in recent times at least, a Royal Forest; certainly, the Commissioners of Woods and Forests have never shown that, officially, it was so considered. Had the neighbouring proprietors been of the opinion that the Crown had any right to Bennachie, doubtless they would have seen to this when the process of division of the Commonty, of which an account is given in the following chapter, was being carried through, so as to prevent the chance of the division being challenged at any future time. The presumption is that, like many other Royal Forests, it had legally and gradually gone to the purchasers of the adjoining lands. The Royal

Forest of Bennachie was anciently the property of the
Earl of Mar, and likely enough went with his other
lands as they were sold or disponed.

The extent of the Commonty, as agreed on by the
neighbouring landlords, was 4042 acres 2 roods
12 poles, but popularly it was of much greater extent.
Indeed, many parts were held as commonty round
about the foot of the hill that gradually were quietly
incorporated in the adjoining estates. On the east it
was bounded by the lands of Pittodrie and Balquhain;
on the south by the lands of Braco, Afforsk, Tillyfour,
and Castle Forbes; on the west by the lands of Castle
Forbes, Leith-hall, and Premnay; and on the north
by the lands of Premnay, Ardoyne, Ryehill, and
Pittodrie. Practically this includes all the hill, but,
perhaps, the reader would prefer, were it only for the
place names, to have the official boundaries as laid
down by the Court of Session in 1859—"On the south
by the Clochie Burn, from the south-east corner of the
said commonty to a point to the west named the
Heather Brig Stone, from that by a curved line
running up the hill north-west, past the ruins of a
smithy, thence westward to the north of Pitgaveny,
across the Howe of the Garbit to a cairn [about
23 chains south-west of Bruntwood Tap, and thus
excluding Millstone Hill], and from the said cairn in
a straight line to the stone of Lang-heather, from that
westward to the Garioch Ford, and from that to the
fir tree and the Peaked Stone [rather less than a
quarter of a mile north of the top of Turf Hill],
through the Star Bog to a cairn at the top of the hill
outside the wood fence belonging to Castle Forbes
marked upon the said plan L C F [about half-a-mile

south-west of the top of Black Hill], and from that due north to the old dyke of Liklyhead, along which to a point marked on the plan L P, and from that along the march of the lands of Premnay contiguous to Lot 2, which is coloured pink on said plan, first nearly due north, and then nearly due east [thus including Black Hill and Hermit Seat], to a point below the hill of Tillymuick [about 12 chains *south* of the top of that hill] marked on the said plan P A, from that eastward along a black dotted line to the point marked L E P on the said plan [excluding the Hill Well and the Fir Park, or Westhall Park], and from that northwards by a march ditch to the old market road [Aberdeen to Insch, &c., already referred to], from thence eastward along the old market road to the gravel pit marked on said plan on the lands of Pittodrie, from thence along the woods of Pittodrie south-westward to a burn [thus including Stay Know], thence eastward to the Bead House marked on the said plan, and from thence southward past Craigna-thunder to a point marked on said plan P B, and from that southwards in a straight line to the Boddach Stone, and from this also southwards past Cairncouly and the Gouk Stone to the Clochy Burn."

There are several interesting names in this descrip-tion. Clochy is more correctly named *Clachie* Burn, deriving the name from its stony channel ; compare Clochnaben and Clachnaben. The Heather Brig is a very unpretentious erection, scarcely noticeable in fact, at the watershed of Birks Burn and Clachie Burn, and likely enough has been made with the assistance of heather. Coming from the east by Clachie Burn or west by Birks Burn, the tourist for the Mither Tap here turns sharply to the north across the Brig. The Heather Brig stone is equally unpretentious, and is on the east side of the Brig, and is marked on the top with the letter A, and on the sides B T. The Garioch Ford is a ford across March Burn, which was much used when cattle and sheep were grazed on the hill. The Boddach (old man) Stone exists no longer, as an enterprising local quarrier looked upon it as a rich prize and quarried it away. (Compare *An Caillach*, the old woman['s stone] in Glen Ey). Cairncouly is a low natural mass of rock and heather on the left as the farthest up farm-house on the north side of Clachie Burn is approached from the east. Close to it, but more to the east, is Kewlie Well. Kewlie and Coulie are probably the same word, the name Coullie is well known both in Monymusk and Udny, and is seen also in *Coull*, another Aberdeenshire parish, and signifies the back-lying place or country. As for the Gouk (Cuckoo) Stone, it is still standing near the left bank of Clachie Burn at the back of an old, roofless—and, perhaps by this time, wall-less house. The stone is somewhat triangularly shaped, the apex standing upward, and on it, it is said, the "gouk" often alighted.

The Commonty was a valuable privilege to the inhabitants of the district, and was freely used by them. Their cattle and sheep were regularly pastured on the hill, the cattle, it is said, having the good sense to come home themselves at night. One squatter was known to have often about 400 sheep on the hill, so there must have been a pretty large number altogether. Fuel, in the shape of peat and turf, was regularly taken from it, though some may think that the expense

of cutting, "setting," and carrying out the peats, and
carting them fully covered their value. Granite stones
and sand, for building; heather, for thatching; and
gravel, composed of disintegrated granite, for roads
were also all taken from the hill. As a "foot-o'-
Bennachie" poet sang (just before the division):

> For the goodly mountain yielded fuel for the fire—
> Stones for the dwelling-house, the barn, and the byre—
> Heather for the roofing, and all were gotten free—
> For no oppressive landlord could swallow Bennachie.

But now all this is changed, and everything that is
removed from the hill has to be paid for. There were
any number of rough cart roads in all directions on
the hill for the due exercise of the rights indicated,
the roads being maintained by those who used them.
In those days there were no "poachers" as the term
is understood now, but the natives regularly shot over
Bennachie as a matter of right.

A great feature of the Commonty was found in the
"squatters." These were of the poorest class, people
with no home, or who, for some good reason, had to
quit their small possessions. Not a few such settled
down on the Commonty, and even on ground unculti-
vated and unused, that, be it observed, strictly
speaking, might not have been "commonty," where
they proceeded, from the materials which they found
pretty much at hand, to build huts or houses for their
own occupation. That was followed up by "rivein'
in a bit grun'" to raise a crop, poor enough often, to
keep them so far in independence with the small
wages they got from the neighbouring farmers for
occasional jobs, together with, in some cases, it must
be said, petty thefts from their more amply-endowed

neighbours. The style of the squatters' houses may be judged from the fact that, on a certain occasion, the neighbours joined together, *and in one day* erected a house for a squatter, celebrating the event by a supper the same evening, in the newly erected building. Thus the squatters lived for a time in a no-man's land, doubtless so far defeating the original idea of a "Commonty," but a terrible day of reckoning came.

Could they be blamed, with their limited intelligence, and fixed belief in the popular rights of commonty, for not seeing the matter in the same light as those who, by and by, claimed to be the proprietors of the habitations their own hands had built (to burn or knock down as they elected), and of the bit of ground they had rescued from nature at the cost of hard and exhausting physical toil? A considerable number had congregated and settled down at the south-east of the Mither Tap on the left bank of Clachie Burn, at a height of about 700 feet, in a spot which ultimately received the name of "the Colony." On the borders of Oyne and Chapel of Garioch, neither parish would admit, when the Poor Law Act came in force, any connection with "the Colony," for the boundary in that neighbourhood was not then very well defined; and it was shrewdly guessed that the "Colonists" would require more assistance from the public funds than they would ever contribute. Ultimately Oyne had to recognise "the Colony" as being within its bounds. The writer once came across a native who was placed in rather a quandary by the action, or rather want of action, of the parochial authorities. The session-clerks of the two contending parishes refused to "proclaim" him on the ground, Chapel of Garioch held, that he resided in Oyne, and Oyne, in Chapel of Garioch. Ultimately the latter proclaimed him as residing in Oyne, Oyne proclaiming him as of Chapel of Garioch !

"The Colony," which once numbered about fifty-five inhabitants, is now a thing of the past, but thirty years have not sufficed to wipe out the marks of houses, gardens, and cultivated fields. Ruins of houses may yet be seen in plenty, still known by the names of their old possessors, and even garden plants and bushes struggle for existence among the trees that have been planted on the sites. The water supply appears to have been ample, almost each house having its "well," in some cases in fair order even at the present day. In going over the sites of the buildings a particular "hen-house" may still be seen that escaped utter demolition, the "nests" in the walls testifying to its use. An old road still exists through "the Colony"; it was the kirk-road for the parishioners in the Tillyfour district of Oyne. South of this road and close to Clachie Burn may still be seen the site of the "Malt Barn," which was used in connection with illicit "whisky running." A little above the "Malt Barn" is a mineral well which was formerly much resorted to, especially on the first Sunday of May. It was believed to be of particular strength and efficacy, and accordingly liberal offerings of pins were made to it.

It is related of a certain "Colonist" that he had a daughter who was so over-diligent in the number of children she added to the population with little consideration as to their fathers, that the clergyman at last demurred to baptising the then latest addition without some particular explanation. The lady did not see her way to meet the church so far, but a "kirsnin'" of some kind being looked upon as essential, her father himself duly performed the ceremony in presence of the neighbours! This was in the time when Rev. Henry Simson, a man of the most estimable character, was parish minister of Chapel of Garioch, and the "Colonist's" name was Beverley. On one occasion he was telling the story of the "kirsnin'" to a worthy mason who was up at the hill looking out for some lintels and other stones. "Aye, man," said the mason, whose sense of humour enabled him to enjoy the situation keenly, "an' fat did ye ca' the creatur'? It's a laddie, ye say." "Fat wud ye think noo, mason?" was Beverley's response. "Oh, I've nae idea." "Ou weel, I gya'im a gweed strong name ony wye. I jist ca'd 'im Samson Eesic [Isaac] Beverley." At a "catechising" the minister asked a young woman, one of the household of a Bennachie squatter, who had recently come from Morayshire, if she knew what the Moral Law was. "Oh, aye!" she replied; "it wis five firlots tae the bowe o' meal fan I wis in Moray, bit I dinna ken fat it is here." (There are *four* firlots in a boll of meal.)

One of the queerest, and perhaps at the same time most undesirable, characters for a neighbour was one William Jamieson, a sort of social outcast, on the Monymusk side. William finally squatted down in the Quarry Smiddy below Garbit Tap, but he had some experiences further down the hill. He lived with several other waifs near Bograxie in such a small hut that, it is said, the inmates had to take turn about

of the bed! Here he was much annoyed by the
youngsters throwing sods down his "lum" at night,
and then running off. William would be at the door
in a second, swearing and cursing at his tormentors,
and crying out, "An' it were daylicht as it's nichtlicht
yer feet shudna cairry ye awa!" His favourite means
of defence, however, was throwing stones, in which,
indeed, he was very liberal, little provocation being
required. He had come across a woman, Mary
Snowie, who set her cap at him. Mary's personal appearance was not very much in her favour, and only a
husband such as William could be looked for. She
led him to understand that there was a cogent reason
why he should marry her forthwith, but Jamieson incontinently took to his heels. He swore he would
"traivel tae unkent pairts," even though he should
have to go "as far as Buchan," but it so happened he
took the south road. He had got as far as the neighbourhood of Montrose, when a crow, sitting on a fence,
said to him, as he used to relate, "Ye'll rue! ye'll
rue!" William took this for a supernatural warning
that he would not thrive unless he turned back and
married Mary Snowie. So he did turn, and was duly
married, but only to find that Mary had deceived him.
Thereafter they settled in the "English" Quarry
Smiddy, and William was frequently called "Toom
Firlots," a name which he reprobated strongly. He
also became known as the "Raven," and the "Heedie
Craw o' Bennachie." The "Heedie Craw" subsisted
pretty much on his neighbours, to whom he was a
great scourge in many ways. He was of an evil disposition, and was continually bringing tenant and
laird into collision, his efforts in that way being

rewarded, it is said, in the larder of Monymusk House. A favourite expression of his, in regard to a certain individual and his business transactions, was, "He's fair, but sair." He was supposed to keep an eye, in his elevated position, on any one who "poached" from the Pittodrie or Logie Elphinstone side on the Monymusk ground. On a particular occasion William was bribed, as he thought, by some sportsmen not to "tell the laird" on them. "A' richt," said Willie; "gin ye dinna tell yersels, nae ither body will." But that was what they forthwith did, with the result that his reputation was considerably damaged where he often got his supplies. He lived about seven years in the old smiddy with his family and died there, Mary afterwards dying in the Poor-house of Oyne.

CHAPTER VI.

THE DIVISION OF THE COMMONTY.

```
A D 1858


   B              P              LĒ
```

This inscription, or ear-marking of Bennachie as it
might fairly be called, which will be found on the top
of the Mither Tap, has puzzled not a few, and
many consider it an unwarranted defacement of the
mountain. The date should be 1859, and the letters
are the initials, respectively, of Balquhain, Pitcaple and
Logie-Elphinstone. This was one of the last acts of
the dividers of Bennachie, the lairds who, agreeing
only among themselves, induced the Court of Session
to divide among them the Commonty of Bennachie.
The lairds had only to put forth their hands and receive
a mountain, the Court taking care that the bigger the
laird the bigger was his share of Bennachie. The public
were no parties to the proceedings; indeed, no one
seems to have thought that they could possibly have any
interest in the partition—nor could even have so much
as whispered a dissentient note.* Nevertheless, if such

---

* A certain gentleman, indeed, in the locality was appealed to
by several on the south side of the hill in the interest of the
public, but nothing was ever done, and it was popularly believed
that he had been ".bribed" by the lairds.

a wholesale "appropriation" were attempted *now* the public would scarcely stand by and allow what was reckoned a "time-immemorial" possession to be divided among half-a-dozen of their number. The division of Bennachie appears legal and final, but there is just a chance that, as Bennachie was long considered a Royal Forest, the fact of the Crown not having been called as a party to the division of the Commonty may yet vitiate the whole proceedings. There is plenty of time to re-open the question—and a re-opening has been talked of frequently—as it will not be till 5th March, 1899, that the landlords will have fortified their position by the uninterrupted possession of the hill for a period of forty years. To many the division of Bennachie seems a stupendous spoliation, a robbery from the public of over four thousand acres—but it would not afford pasturage for a rabbit compared to the great slices of Scotland quietly, and without any legal process, appropriated by the large landowners who had some of the greatest mountains of our country within their grasp. One needs not go further than the south-western corner of Aberdeenshire to see examples of how men have yielded to the cravings of an all-consuming "yird-hunger."

The neighbouring lairds were not altogether a happy family, as, for more than a century before the final process was taken in Court to divide Bennachie, there were occasional bickerings as to their individual rights in the commonty. Over a hundred years ago, when the estate of Braco belonged to the Earl of Aberdeen, an attempt was made at a division, a tent even having been set up on the eastern slope of the Mither Tap for holding an informal "court" on the subject.

Apparently there was then a process between the
Lairds of Balquhain and Pittodrie and the Earl of
Aberdeen as Proprietor of the lands of Braco, as
certain papers in the Pittodrie charter-chest show.
One of these papers is a protest at the instance of
Captain James Leslie of Pitcaple, Heir of Entail of
Balquhain, and Erskine of Pittodrie, and is dated 7th
June, 1740. It protests against the Earl and his
tenants for casting peats "in that part of the Moss of
Bend-up-high commonly called the head of the Bod-
dach," but the matter was ultimately mutually adjusted.
On 21st February, 1844, an action for the division of
the Commonty was raised by the then proprietor of
the estate of Logie-Elphinstone, Sir Robert Dalrymple
Horn Elphinstone, Baronet, who, it may be mentioned
incidentally, was laughed at by the natives for endea-
vouring to accomplish what, to them in their ignorance,
seemed impossible. On 18th July, 1845, the Court of
Session found he had a title to proceed with the action,
and granted a commission to Mr. John Thomson
Gordon for taking evidence. Then, on 6th February,
1846, a "common agent," Mr. Arthur Forbes, afterwards Mr. Arthur Forbes Gordon, W.S., was appointed
to conduct the "process" for behoof of all the parties
interested. On 4th June, 1847—observe how deliber-
ately justice proceeds with her work—all claims on
Bennachie were ordered to be sent in. In October,
1847, proof was taken at Pitcaple Inn (now shut up as
already mentioned), as being the most convenient
place, alike for the parties and their witnesses. This
proof was held for two purposes—(1) the production
of the titles of the landlords, and an examination of
the rights thereby given; and (2) the examination of

witnesses as to how long and to what extent the rights—rights of pasturing cattle and sheep, casting peats, divots, and feal, quarrying stones, and shooting game—had been exercised.

In 1845 the lairds had a plan prepared, which was lithographed by Maclure & Macdonald, Glasgow. It is titled :—" Reduced Plan of the Common of Beinna-chie, Lying in the Parishes of Chapel of Garioch, Oyne, and Premnay, and County of Aberdeen. Surveyed by Alexander Smith, [afterwards the author of 'A New History of Aberdeenshire,'] 1845." The extent of the "Common" is there given as 4472 acres 3 roods 29 poles, but in 1846, by agreement of parties, 430 acres 1 rood 17 poles, held to be the sole property of the Baronet of Logie Elphinstone, were taken off, thus leaving 4042 acres 2 roods 12 poles, the boundaries of which were defined and agreed to on 17th February, 1847. In July, 1849, the lairds interested agreed among themselves that pending the division a "watcher" should be engaged on the hill to protect their interests.

It was not till the year 1852, however, that the Commissioner submitted "notes" to the parties with a view to his "report." These "notes" met the approval of all except Colonel Leslie of Balquhain, but he was "squared" by the laird of Tillyfour, and accordingly withdrew his objections. So the "notes" duly blossomed into a "draft report" in June, 1853, and into a "report" submitted to the First Division on 18th January, 1854. But Auchindoir had some slight objections to the report, which he succeeded in getting his brother lairds to listen to. Then a joint minute was agreed to, and the Lord Ordinary (Neaves) pronounced, on 20th July, 1854, an interlocutor settling

various points, and remitting to "James Forbes
Beattie, land surveyor in Aberdeen, and valuator of
lands, with instructions . . . First to perambulate
and go over the whole Commonty with a view to
ascertaining the quality of its different parts, in order
to its division . . . second, to value separately
the rights of servitude of pasturage and usage of taking
stones, found to have been established by the various
parties ; and third, to prepare such valuations and
statements of the value of the different portions of the
Commonty as may enable him to carry into effect the
Judgment of the Lord Ordinary or the Court. . . ."

Little time was lost by Mr. Beattie in preparing his
report to the Court, which bears date 14th December,
1854. It was afterwards amended in some points,
but, as it was the foundation of the decision of the
Court of Session (First Division), it is an interesting
document, so I quote several passages from it :

"Report by James Forbes Beattie in the Remit by Lord
     Ordinary Neaves in the Process of Division of the Com-
     monty of Bennachie.

Having, in terms of your Lordship's Interlocutor and Remit
. . . . perambulated the whole Commonty, for the purpose
of ascertaining the quality of its different parts, and having well
considered the terms of the Commissioner's Report of the 18th
January, 1854, as to the principle of the division of the different
parts, and also taken into consideration the right of servitudes of
pasturage and the usage of taking stones, as established by the
several parties, I beg to report :—

First—That the common lands comprise a mountain range of
about 3½ miles long by 2 miles wide, containing 4042 im-
perial acres or thereby.   The ridge of the mountain is broken
by several peaks or summits of granite rock, boldly thrown up
through a stratum of clay, intimately mixed with decomposed
granite in various stages, and the surface presents a rough,

strong, and rocky moor inferior in pasturage. The different parts are so mixed and blended together that it is impossible to report accurately the extent or quality of the parts by definite outlines.

The lower portion of the slopes . . . . comprises the better description of pasturage. The remainder or higher portion contains the rocky and most stony parts, also the moss ; and I am of opinion that the value of the pasturage here is about one half less per acre than that on the lower slopes, and by adopting this principle I consider that a fair division of the lands could be carried out.

The moss extends over a part of the table-land of the mountain . . . . and varies from 2 to 7 feet deep generally, but some spots may exceed 7 feet deep.

. . . Stones are found over the whole surface, excepting where covered by the deep moss. These surface or outlying stones are in some places in greater quantity and of more value than others, but they chiefly lie along the slopes near the base of the rocky peaks, and on the highest leading ridges.

The usage of taking stones hitherto has been exercised only in the removal of the best outlying surface stones, but a vast supply of stones can be obtained from the masses of solid rock, and equally accessible by roads, as the surface stones.

Second—With regard to the value of the rights of servitude of pasturage, and the usage of taking stones :—

The servitude of pasturage implies a breadth of surface of ground, and would fall to be included in the division of the common lands with the right of common property, and by following the principle recommended in the Commissioner's Report of allowing four-fifths of the valued rents of the lands possessing the right of pasturage to be ranked under the head of common property, this right would be, in my opinion, fairly adjusted in the division of the common lands.

The usage of taking stones does not imply the necessity of allocating a breadth of surface of ground for that purpose.

Those parties receiving their proportion of the common lands to correspond with the amount of their valued rents in right of common property and servitudes of pasturage would necessarily embrace in their respective divisions a due proportion of the stones to satisfy their right of that usage ; at all events the lines of division of the common lands can be adjusted to include stones and rock to supply them amply in that respect. . . . In regard to the servitudes of fuel, and the usage of taking feal and divot and heather :—

The Moss applicable or valuable for division as fuel lies on the table-land of the mountain, in one continued space, and is so situated as to admit of a fair division according to its quality and depth, and the means of access to it in proportion to the valued rents of the lands to which the right of fuel has been recognised, and as the moss is worked off, the land or solum will fall to the proprietor on whose division the moss may happen to be placed.

The usage of taking feal and divot and heather is not now exercised by those at a distance having the right, nor can it be given effect to in carrying out a convenient and beneficial division of the lands.

Roads to the moss, and the various divisions of the Commonty, will have to be secured to the parties. At present access is afforded by a road from the west, and one from the east, two from the north, and one from the south, and it appears to me that an equal number will in future be required.

Third—The adoption of the amount of the valued rents of the lands belonging to the respective parties whose claims have been recognised seems to be a fair principle of division for the right of common property, and by assuming 4-5ths of the valued rents on the servitude of pasturage as equal to the right of common property. I am of opinion that a just principle of division could then be carried out, as well for the lands as for the division of the fuel. . . . ."

On 2nd March, 1855, the Lord Ordinary issued an interlocutor ordering Mr. Beattie to lodge a scheme of division. Objections were, however, given in to this scheme on its being lodged, and a new scheme was ordered in 1857. Mr. Beattie's final scheme was reported to the Court on 20th January, 1858, and agreed to, Mr. Beattie being directed to set march stones and cairns for the division and to set the peat mosses. The Commonty was thus divided :

Estates.	Proprietors.	Acs.	Rds.	Pls.
Ardoyne	Robert Grant (1)	327	2	18
Auchindoir	Henry Lumsden (2)	910	2	29
Balquhain	Colonel Leslie (3)..............	316	3	25
Castle Forbes......	Lord Forbes (4)	133	0	0
Leith-hall...........	Sir Andrew Leith Hay and Son (5)..	335	0	0
Logie-Elphinstone	Sir J. D. H. Elphinstone (6)	872	0	25
Monymusk	Sir James Grant (7)............	71	2	15
Pittodrie	Colonel Erskine (8)............	655	2	20
Tillyfour	Trustees of Robert Grant (9)	420	0	0
Total		4042	2	12

(1) In respect of his lands of Buchanstone, Ardoyne, and Hatton ; also for right of servitude in respect of his lands of Ardoyne.

(2) In respect of his lands of Premnay, &c. ; also for right of servitude in respect of his lands of Harlaw.

(3) In respect of his lands of Balquhain, Whitecross, and Tulloch ; also for right of servitude in respect of his lands of Aulton, Nethertown, and Middleton of Knockenlewis.

(4) In respect of his lands of Puttachie, including Glentowns and Auchterkeig, &c. ; also for right of servitude in respect of his lands of Pittendreich, Tulloch, Tinzeach, and Kincraigie.

(5) In respect of their lands of Edingarioch and Brindy, Auchnagathel, &c. ; also for right of servitude in respect of their lands of Leslie, Flindars, &c.

(6) In respect of his lands of Westhall, Ryehill, including part of Buchanstone, Raetirs, and Mill of Carden ; also for rights of servitude in respect of his lands of Pitcaple's Plough (part of the lands of Ardoyne), Pitmedden, and Logie-Elphinstone.

(7) In respect of his lands of Afforsk, &c.

(8) In respect of his lands of Newlands, Kirktown, Torris, Carden, Harthill, and Old Harthill ; also for right of servitude in respect of his lands of Drumdurno, Dorlethen, &c.

(9) In respect of the lands of Tillyfour and Braco.

Included in the acreage above given, the proprietors had reserved to them a certain part of the moss on the Logie-Elphinstone and Tillyfour divisions

H

(principally on the former), the *solum* to revert to these estates on the exhaustion of the moss. Thus Bennachie was parted, but moss, as under, was also reserved on the same divisions in respect of rights of servitude only :

		Acs.	Rds.	Pls.
Balgowan...........	Trustees of R. C. Grant......	5	0	0
Drimmies.	Alexander Sharp Shand......	1	2	20
Drumrossie.........	William Leslie..................	4	1	20
	Keig, Logie-Durno, and Premnay Ministers and Schoolmasters....................	1	3	0
Overhall............	Theodore Gordon	5	2	0
Pitcaple	Hugh Lumsden......	3	1	0

The *solum* on the exhaustion of the moss thus set apart reverts to Logie-Elphinstone and Tillyfour as in the other cases. The interlocutor settling the division is dated 5th March, 1859—fifteen years after the proceedings commenced. This was an end of the matter, except the question of the " common" expenses. These appear to have amounted to £1021 7s. 2d., and were proportionally divided among the nine lairds, a trifle of £63 1s. 10-7-12d. of the above being debited to the five proprietors in the last list, the ministers and schoolmasters being graciously allowed to escape scot free. With the "common" and the individual expenses, the division must have been rather a costly matter—not less, probably, than £1 per acre.

It is, of course, impossible to show the portions of Bennachie allotted to the nine proprietors severally without a plan, but a rough idea of the division can be had from the following description :

Ardoyne—Hummel Craig and the north-east part of Watch Craig.

Auchindoir — Hermit's Seat and the remainder of
Watch Craig.

Balquhain—The south part of the Mither Tap.

Castle Forbes—A small triangular strip to the west of
March Burn, along the foot of Auchindoir and
Leith-hall's shares.

Leith-hall—Black Hill.

Logie-Elphinstone—Oxen Craig, Little Oxen Craig,
Craig Shannoch, Moss Grieve, and the north side
of Garbit Tap—a division which called forth the
rhyme :

> Bennachie, the landmark's
> Noo but a pimple,
> Stickin' o' the nose
> O' Sir James Dalrymple.

Monymusk—A small strip south of and between the
Mither Tap and Garbit Tap.

Pittodrie—The north-east part of the Mither Tap,
Nether Maiden, Hosie's Well, Little John's
Length, and Stay Know.

Tillyfour—The south part of Garbit Tap, Bruntwood
Tap, and along to March Burn.

As a local poet wailed :

> Oh ! ye was ance a monarch hill,
> To freedom's footsteps free ;
> But noo, unless their honours will,
> We daurna tread on thee.
> Alas ! the heather on thy broo
> Will bloom nae mair for me ;
> The lairds aroon' hae ta'en ye noo—
> Ye're nae oor Bennachie.

The partition was sullenly assented to by most
of the natives, for no open opposition dared be
given, but the "Squatters" and "Colonists" were

for some time a source of annoyance to the lairds.
They were not, perhaps, in some cases, desirable
neighbours, as a byword—"as great a thief as there
is in a' the Backhill o' Pittodrie"—bears witness ; but
still they were human, and burning their roofs over their
heads was doubtless as painful and inconvenient to
them as similar burnings were to the tenants of many
a Highland glen when called on to make room for
deer. A certain eviction was a particularly trying and
disheartening operation to one family. The guidwife
had just got the interior of her house nicely done up,
according to the then fashion, and bought a "kist
o' drawers" to add to the humble furnishings, and
on the following day the house was pulled down.
Some of the "Colonists," from age and other in-
firmities, had to be carried out. Several crofters
also continued taking peats, &c. from the hill
in spite of all threats of interdict, and more than
once some persons, in revenge for their supposed
rights being usurped, set fire to the heather. The
neighbouring laird of Cluny was wont to have an
annual "hunt" on the hill, which he did not discon-
tinue on the division. But even he at last subsided,
for, when it was known he was about to shoot, men
were sent out in advance by the proprietors armed with
tin pails, pans, girdles, &c. to make such a clamour as
would frighten off the game. One sturdy "lover of
sport," who used to go out with his gun, also persisted
after the decree of '59, but it is said a good dinner
from Sir James D. H. Elphinstone brought about even
his submission ! Gradually all gave way to the new
order of things, and the Commonty was no more.
But in any event a time would soon have come when

its abuse would have been legally ended by the public. It may, indeed, be safely asserted that under no circumstances will the *status quo* be resumed, for the public does not particularly desire that a certain few, be they squatters or landlords, should have the exclusive right of building houses and enclosing ground on Bennachie for individual use. As I take it, what the public really want is that all should be free of the hill as a place of public resort, the present legal owners still having the sole right of game and property—for so long at least as the law may recognise private rights whether in mountain or in field.

CHAPTER VII.

THE MAIDEN STONE.

The Maiden Stone, which is one of the most remarkable and noted of the standing stones of the north of Scotland, is still a puzzle to antiquaries. Much has been written about it, both from a legendary and an antiquarian point of view, and many a journey has been taken to Bennachie with the view of inspecting the ancient monolith. Naturally it has found a place in "The Sculptured Stones of Scotland," published by the Spalding Club, as well as in other less pretentious works. The late Rev. John Longmuir, LL.D., Aberdeen, in particular, wrote a pamphlet (1869) on the subject, of which I have availed myself in the present chapter.

The Maiden Stone stands on the farm of Drumdurno, in the parish of Chapel of Garioch, about half-a-mile north-west of the Church; about two miles south-west of Pitcaple Station, and the same distance north-east from the Mither Tap, so much associated with it in the legendary versions of its origin. More than likely the stone itself had at some remote time come from the neighbourhood of the Tap, for it is composed of the same coarse reddish granite that prevails all over Bennachie. It stands nearly erect with a slight inclination to the west-north-west, and it is embedded in the ground to the supposed depth of six feet. The height, from the commencement of the dressing, is

10 feet 6 inches; the breadth, immediately above the first compartment, is 2 feet 10 inches; the thickness at the same place being 12 inches, but the breadth and thickness diminish somewhat towards the top. The triangular slope near the ground had resulted from a fracture in the dressing, and had been covered by an ornamental knot. A similar angular piece, but near the top, has been subsequently broken out of the same side, which had been the more easily done in consequence of a "dry," parallel to that where the fracture had taken place below. Above the ornamental fracture is the broad arrow of the Ordnance Survey, the horizontal line on which is at a height of 517·5 feet above the mean level of the sea at Liverpool.

The stone faces the east-south-east and west-north-west. The easterly side inclines a little upwards, and is divided into four compartments, which I shall briefly describe. The four compartments are divided by a rod-like moulding that also runs along the edges, each containing one or more figures in relief. Beginning at the upper compartment, which is considerably mutilated through the irregularities produced by time or accident, we perceive portions of four quadrupeds that are not easily defined. The hind-quarters of the lower and larger one exhibit considerable spirit and accuracy of drawing, but it is almost impossible to determine the nature of the head. Dr. Longmuir came to the conclusion that it was a centaur, undoubted examples of which are to be found in several other standing stones in the north of Scotland. The centaur is also found on the earliest British coins, as well as on those of ancient Greece. In the next compartment is a figure which by some is

EAST SIDE.   WEST SIDE.

THE MAIDEN STONE.

called the "oblong ornament," by others a "fire altar," but it is also suggested that it is the cross section or end of a throne. The third compartment contains the figure of an elephant, with the trunk cast over the head, that being believed to be the technical and traditional, or conventional, form of representation. Indian monuments show elephants similarly sculptured. The elephant was naturally emblematical of a great man, but, according to some, of the spirit of the earth. The fourth compartment contains two figures, concerning which there is no dispute—a mirror and a comb. The former was doubtless metallic, the latter probably wooden, ancient mirrors of a similar shape having been found in Scotland. Both the mirror and comb were common deposits in ancient graves, and have been found sculptured on Roman tombs as well as on standing stones in Scotland, and are unquestionably symbolical of the female sex. The natural conclusion, therefore, is that the Maiden Stone is rightly so called, being most probably the monument of some distinguished woman. Distinguished she must have been, for the emblems negative any other assumption, and, besides, the expense of such a piece of work precludes an ordinary "daughter of the soil" from having been so honoured.

On the westerly side, which inclines a little downwards, there are only two compartments, the lower having a moulding. The figures are scarcely traceable to an unpractised eye, and they are yearly becoming more and more obscure. Whether this defacement arises from this side of the stone being softer than the other, or from the sculptures having been lower in relief, or executed at a

different time, is not easy to determine. The outline of
the lower figure is a circle, whose diameter occupies almost the breadth of the stone; then there is an inner con-
centric circle, whose diameter is somewhat more than
half that of the outer; a spiral ornament, not unknown
on other stones, occupies the centre; and the ring
has been ornamented, as we may infer from some
remaining fragments, with the well-known zig-zag or
wicker-work pattern. Each of the lower corners is
filled with a simple knot, and each of the upper with
one somewhat more complicated. Above this circular
figure, but separated from it by a moulding, stands a
Cross, which has likewise been ornamented, as well
as the space between its stem and the edges of the
stone, probably with the wicker-work pattern, but it is
impossible to trace the design. The stem of the Cross
is a little more than five feet high and one foot broad;
the short arms extend to the edges of the stone; and
the angles of intersection are rounded off by the usual
circle, which is here indicated by little more than four
oval hollows at the angles above and below the arms
of the Cross. The wicker-work pattern is accounted
for by the extensive use of willow by the early inhabitants of Britain, wicker-work being used in the
construction of their houses, boats, shields, baskets,
palaces, churches, &c., not to mention the huge frame
made of osiers in which criminals and other victims
were burned to death. The circle joining the arms of
the Cross, therefore, must have been suggested by the
willow cross, a circle being necessary to keep the
horizontal arm of the latter in position. But the Cross
is almost unique in being surmounted by a circle, the
raison d'etre of which has given rise to much dis-

cussion and research. The spaces above the transverse part are occupied by what at first sight might be taken for a pair of brackets supporting the circle, and terminating in a scroll. Within this circle there was a figure like a man standing on the top of the Cross, but a recent exfoliation has removed every trace of it. It has been suggested that the scrolls might be the terminations of some grotesque animals, and on a minute examination being made the head and fore-leg of an animal were found on the left of the circle.

As to the local traditions concerning the origin of this stone, none must be looked at seriously, but all are interesting. In "Don, a Poem," published in London in 1655, and reprinted in Aberdeen in 1797, written by the schoolmaster of Premnay, there is the following note : " Betwixt Pittodry and Chapel is the Maiden Stone, of which so many fabulous stories are told ; but I suppose it has been a march betwixt the Earls of Mar and Buchan, and the figure of a woman and bread-girdle represent the Garioch as the Land of Cakes, as everybody knows that the Garioch has often been called the Meal Girnal of Aberdeen." " The Statistical Account of Aberdeenshire," 1843, says the occasion of its erection is unknown, but there is a tradition that there existed a feud betwixt the Laird of Balquhain and the neighbouring proprietor of Harthill, which was carried to such a height that they had no intercourse with each other. Notwithstanding this, it is reported that the daughter of the former and the son of the latter became attached to each other. Upon an appointed day the young people set off together, when their flight being immediately communicated to the Laird of Balquhain, he pursued them with as many of his vassals as he could collect, and, having overtaken the fugitives at the place where the stone is erected, a rencontre took place, in which the young lady was unfortunately killed. Afterwards this stone was erected to her memory, and from hence called the Maiden Stone.

Moyse's "Memoirs of the Family of Leslie" gives a more circumstantial account. Andrew Leslie, fifth Baron of Balquhain, in 1419, carried off Isabella Mortimer, and married her, which incited her father to seek revenge. Lord Forbes of Drumminor and Sir James Stewart of Inveraven espoused the cause of Mortimer. Balquhain, seeing how matters ran, withdrew from the castle, and abode on a neighbouring mountain called Bennachie, where he remained secure in his old fortress. The Mortimers, Stewarts, and Forbeses formed innumerable schemes to lure him from his retreat. At last, after assembling a few friends, he came down to the valley and gave them battle. Lady Leslie threw herself between the combatants, entreating them to stop the carnage. Here Balquhain fell with some of his vassals on 23rd January, 1420. On the ground is seen a flat stone, sculptured with hieroglyphics, called Leslie's Cross. The stone measures above ground ten feet in height, in thickness fourteen inches, and in breadth twenty-eight inches. It is vulgarly called the Maiden Stone, and report circulates tales of it quite grating to the human ear. On the upper compartment of the stone are the words Swiftness and Strength, represented by a horse courant. Under this are the words Valour and Victory, signified by a cross and two spears. In the third compartment is an elephant rampant, figurative of Courage, Royalty, and Sagacity; and in the last a shield and book, emblems of Faith and Fortitude. "With strength we bounded on to battle, swift as the mountain roe, our hearts beating with courage, our bosoms glowing with faith, and, through the standard of the Cross, we were victorious!"

This latter account and explanation seems now rather ridiculous, and one wonders how it could ever have passed current. The "fortress" of Balquhain on Bennachie—doubtless the Mither Tap fortification, at once, I think, makes an end of the Leslie Cross theory, not to mention the utter absurdity of taking the mirror and comb on the stone for a shield and book. The legend then considered "grating to the human ear" may now be briefly given:

The Maiden of Drumdurno, as the daughter of the farmer of Drumdurno was called, was the belle of five parishes. She was young and light-hearted, and suitors came round her in plenty, for she was a bit of a coquette—a coquetry which afterwards cost her life. Ultimately one was fortunate enough in gaining her heart, and was received as her acknowledged lover. Her unsuccessful wooers retired disappointed, but all, with *one* exception, wished her long life and happiness. For in the heart of one of the rejected suitors there brooded thoughts of vengeance, and as he wandered on a certain evening by the dark woods of Pittodrie, thinking bitterly of his successful rival, he exclaimed aloud, "Oh that my eternal destruction could plague their earthly peace, how soon and sure the bargain would be mine!" Scarcely had he uttered the rash words when the Enemy of Mankind made answer; "Capital wish! I'll do the thing for

you on your own terms," and the bargain was at once
concluded.   On the day before the wedding the
Maiden was busy baking cakes for the bridal feast, and
as she baked she gaily lilted one of the love songs
of the district.   " It sets ye weel to bake, lass, gin ye
had ony mair speed at it."   This bantering remark
was made by a handsome rollicking stranger as he
entered the "kitchie."   "I kenna whether it sets me
weel or no," replied the maiden ; "but I think nane
could grudge my speed."   After some further banter,
the stranger undertook to lay a " causey " to the top of
the Mither Tap of Bennachie before she had finished
her firlot, on the condition that, if successful, her
hand and heart should be his reward.   Deeming it a
piece of idle fun, the lassie thoughtlessly agreed to the
proposal, whereupon the stranger went on his way, and
the baker resumed her task.   Twilight drew on apace,
and the firlot of meal was nearly ended, but the
stranger and his wager were forgotten, the bride
thinking only of her Jamie, who had promised to call
on her in the gloaming.   The evening came down
gloomy and wet, and as the Maiden of Drumdurno
looked out for her betrothed she observed the clouds
gather on Bennachie, and, alas ! a well finished
"causey" up the slope of the Mither Tap.*   At the

---

*One incident, illustrative of the stiff fight Satan had to find
the necessary material rapidly enough to enable him to finish the
causey in time to win his prey, must not be omitted.   All the
stones lying handy being used up, "his wife," who had been
acting as "labourer," had gone down as far as Pennan for an
"awpron fraucht."   And coming hastily up with her burden,
the apron strings gave way when she had reached the upper part
of the parish of Monkeggie (or Keith-hall), the stones, which fell
with a "doisht" to the earth, forming a hill of some extent.

same moment she beheld the stranger, who, as she
now discovered, was no other than the Prince of
Darkness, quickly and noiselessly coming to claim his
reward. She instantly fled towards the Pittodrie woods
hoping to meet her Jamie, or some one who might
save her from his black majesty. Poor girl! there
was no earthly help at hand, and as the stranger was
about to clasp her in his arms, she was turned, in
response to an exclamation for help from heaven, into
a block of lifeless granite, and accordingly there she
stands to this day. In truth of this tradition the
"causey" may still be seen, and on the stone her *bake
brod* and *bread spade* indelibly printed on her apron,
and a piece of the stone is wanting where the Maiden
had been seized by the foul fiend!

Dr. Longmuir's rhyme of the Legend will, I think,
suitably close this chapter :

THE MAIDEN OF DRUMDURNO;

OR,

A LEGEND OF THE MAIDEN STONE.

> Busy baking for her bridal,
>   Durno's maiden lilts with glee,
> When a roader, handsome, idle,
>   Saunters in, and thus says he—
> " Baking sets you well indeed,
>   If you made but greater speed ! "

There they lay, and, when the Flood was in full swing, the Ark,
happening to come that way, stuck on the top of this very hill ;
whereat Noah, looking out, told it to "sail-by." And behold
the hill is known as " the hill of Selby " to this day !

[This foot-note is by the Editor of the *Aberdeen Weekly Free
Press*, in which paper "Bennachie," since re-arranged and partly
re-written, originally appeared.]

Gaily she retorts his banter—
    " Little care I how I bake ;
But, though I dislike a vaunter,
    Few could blame the speed I make."
Scornfully she toss'd her head,
And another bannock spread.

" Quick or slowly—fair and saucy—
    Ere your firlot's end you see,
I engage to lay a causey
    Up the craigs of Bennachie,
If, should I the contest gain,
I your heart and hand obtain !"

She, on such a foolish wager,
    Lightly granted what he ask'd ;
He, like an undaunted stager,
    Dared what had a legion task'd.
Stone to stone ascends the slope ;
Quick is labour cheered by hope.

Now her work of love is closing,
    And the lavrock's song is still ;
Day, her dewy wings composing,
    Leaves the gloaming on the hill ;
Mary, with a fieldward glance,
Chides her Jamie's slow advance.

What arrests her eye so glassy,
    Makes her glowing cheek turn pale ?
Can that be a well-laid causey
    Stretching upwards from the vale ?
Must a lightly-spoken jest
Tear her from her Jamie's breast ?

Near the roader's step is stealing,
    Noiseless as the backie's wing ;
Now she sees that road revealing
    Him who flatters but to sting,
Fast she flies, as fast pursued,
Straining for Pittodrie Wood.

" Jamie !" shrieks the frantic maiden,
   As he wildly scours the hill,
But a heavy hand is laid on
   Mary's arm ; her heart is still.
Traitor, now the maiden clasp !
Now the lifeless granite grasp !

Lone and last of all the *clachan*,
   With her *bake-brod* and *bread-spade*,
Aye she bids the maids of Buchan
   Guard the vows that love has made.
Love is holy, love is solemn !
Think of this mysterious column !

I

CHAPTER VIII.

THE GARIOCH.

Bennachie is the mountain of the Garioch, so a little in the way of general notice of this division of the county may now fitly be given.

Aberdeenshire was anciently divided into five great districts, viz., Buchan on the north, Mar on the south-west, and Formartine, Garioch, and Strathbogie in the middle. These divisions are still more or less familiarly in use. Anciently Garioch was an earldom and an appanage of the King, being held by the Earl of Mar ; now the sole connection between that dignity and the district is that the latter gives the title of Lord Garioch to the eldest son of Lord Mar. The Garioch is now best known as a fertile district of the county, and the name of a Presbytery embracing the following fifteen parishes : Bourtie, Chapel of Garioch, Culsalmond, Daviot, Insch, Inverurie, Keith-hall and Kinkell, Kemnay, Kintore, Leslie, Meldrum, Monymusk, Oyne, Premnay, and Rayne. Garioch is a Gaelic word, signifying the rough district, as it had doubtless once been, though it ultimately acquired the local designation of the meal girnal or granary of Aberdeenshire.

The first seat of Christianity in the Garioch, and among the first in the North, was at Monymusk, where the Culdees had a settlement. Malcolm Canmore passed through the parish in 1078 on his way to suppress the rebels in Moray, and vowed a priory while

there should he be successful. Having been successful he duly kept his vow, and a portion of the priory
yet forms part of the Parish Church of Monymusk.
When the Culdees were dispossessed the Canons
Regular of St. Andrews received their lands, and the
Bishop of St. Andrews sat in the Scottish Parliament
as Lord Keig and Monymusk.

In pre-historic times Bennachie had, according to
Rev. Dr. Davidson, Inverurie, overlooked the great
lake of the Garioch, which had come up as far, on the
one hand, as Putachie (Castle Forbes), and, on the
other, to the meeting of the Gadie and the Ury (Logie
Elphinstone).

There is an old rhyme, of doubtful signification,
concerning the Garioch, Mar, and Bennachie. It
runs thus :

> The Grole o' the Garioch,
> The Bowman o' Mar,
> Upon the hill o' Bennachie
> The Grole wan the war.

It is also met with in the following form :

> The Gweel o' the Garioch
> And the Bowman o' Mar
> Met on the tap o' Bennachie,
> The Gweel wan the war.

"Gweel" is familiar in Strathspey from the following
couplet :

> The Gweel, the Gordon, an' the Heedie Craw
> Are the three warst en'mies Moray ever saw.

"Gweel" or "Guil" (*Chrysanthemum segetum*, corn
marygold, or yellow ox-eye) is a well-known plant
which infests the fields in some districts, and is so
called from its gold or golden ("guile" or guilden)
colour; "The Gordon" is the Gordon family; and the

"Heedie Craw" (hooded crow) refers to the old Churchmen or Monks with their hoods.

The latter form of the quatrain shows the unsuccessful effort made by the "bowman" or "bollman"—the old name for farmer—of the district of Mar to keep out the Garioch-flourishing weed "gweel." On the other hand, some hold "grole" to be closely allied to *groat* or *grout*—large or very round oatmeal—and girnal, a large meal chest, to be of the same derivation. Hence "grole" might be taken for the man who had charge of the girnal, and "bowman" or "bollman" would thus be another term for the same person, from *bow* or *boll*, a Scotch meal measure. Thus the stanza in its first form might be rendered as meaning that the Garioch and Mar districts contended over their corn-growing capabilities on Bennachie, the prominent division line between the two districts, and that the Grole (personifying the Garioch) won the war—in other words, that the Garioch was found to be a better corn-producing district than Mar. But there are good authorities who will not allow that "Grole" has any connection with a yellow weed or meal, and who hold that it should be spelled "Growl." In that case it refers to the chief man on the other side of the hill, who, from his expertness with the bow, was called the Bowman of Mar, and was met on Bennachie and got the worst of it—in other words, did not win the war.

Fairies, in popular belief, were to be found in the Garioch, and particularly about Bennachie, and, as in other places, were spoken of with respect by the inhabitants of the district. Certain fairies dwelt in the neighbourhood of the Hill Park, and were of a particularly benevolent disposition, though at times

they played sad tricks with the rustics. The story is
yet told how two ploughmen, on their way to the
"smiddy" with their "socks," came on a number of
them dancing, and were entranced at the sight. One
of the ploughmen, however, managed to tear himself
away, but his companion seemed a fixture, for he was
not seen till a year and a day afterwards, when his
friend passing by the same place so far had his eyes
opened as to see him standing, mouth open, intently
watching something. On being asked to come along,
he replied, as though he had only been there for a few
minutes, that he would rather wait a little yet! And
there he still stands—at anyrate he was never seen
again.

The winding Don is the river of the Garioch,
it or its tributaries flowing through all its parishes.
Besides, it is also the river of Bennachie, for it is
drained by it alone—on the south side by the river
directly; and on the north through the Water of
Gadie, which, united with the Ury, joins the Don near
Inverurie. From the two chief tops of Bennachie the
long winding hollow through which the Don flows,
and the watershed bounding its basin, may be traced
in many parts from Corgarff to near the sea.

Popularly the Don is considered the twin-sister
river of the Dee, but the differences between the two
rivers are really so great that I think the relationship
cannot be considered nearer than cousin-ship. It has
a course of about 82 miles, rising on the Brown Cow
Hill and the Geal Charns on the borders of Aberdeenshire and Banffshire, near Loch Builg and Inchrory
on the Avon. In the Garioch, it flows through
or along Monymusk, Oyne, Chapel of Garioch,

Kemnay, Inverurie, Keith-hall and Kinkell, and Kintore ; and, indeed, the prettiest part of the Don is,
I think, that between Keig and Inverurie, in its wind-
ings through a well wooded plain between two as
finely wooded hollows.

There are several old couplets in which the Don is
referred to :

> A mile o' Don's worth twa o' Dee,
> Excep' for sa'mon, stane, and tree.

> A mile o' Don's worth twa o' Dee,
> For horn, corn, fish, and tree.

> Don and Deveron for grass and corn,
> Spey and Dee for fish and tree.

> A foot o' Don's worth twa o' Dee,
> Except it be for fish and tree.

This explains the difference pretty tersely between
the rivers. The Don drains a basin of 530 square miles,
70 less than the Dee. It is a capital trouting river,
especially in the upper reaches. Thomas the Rhymer
has the following prophecy :

> When Dee and Don run both in one,
>   And Tweed shall run in Tay,
> Ye little water o' Ury
>   Shall bear ye Bass away.

The first line is sometimes given thus :

> The Dee and Don shall run in one.

And another version has it :

> The Dee an' Don shall still run on,
>   An' Tweed shall run and Tay,
> But the bonnie water o' Ury
>   Shall bear the Bass away.

The legend is that, but for artificial defences, the

Bass would have been borne away. The Dee and Don did partly run in one when the Aberdeenshire Canal (from Port Elphinstone to Aberdeen) was opened in 1807, not to mention the time when the Don is said to have flowed across the Old Aberdeen and Aberdeen Links, and joined the Dee a little short of the sea. There is a proverb, " He has as many crooks as Don," referring to its winding course. The Bennachie portion of the Don is crossed by four bridges—Keig, Castle Forbes (foot), Ramstone (foot), and Kemnay.

CHAPTER IX.

THE GADIE.

"Bennachie" suggests "Gadie," and "Gadie" suggests "Bennachie," so closely are the two names popularly connected together. This arises, doubtless, from the popularity of the songs about the Gadie, for it must be confessed that, viewed as a burn simply, the Gadie is not such a beautiful stream as might fairly be expected from its almost world-wide reputation. Not that it is *not* a beautiful stream, only I think it is a *little* over-rated, though between the Churches of Premnay and Leslie there is a loneliness about the banks of the stream well fitted for poetic meditation within ear of the song of the lark and the crow of the grouse. The Gadie songs have probably made Bennachie more famous than Byron's stanzas have made Lochnagar.

The Gadie is wholly a Garioch stream, and rises in the parish of Clatt—on the east side of the watershed of the Water of Bogie. It has a course of about 13 miles, and is a fair trouting stream, salmon coming up only to spawn. From Clatt it flows through the parish of Leslie, past the old Castle of Leslie, through Premnay to the village of Auchleven and the Church of Premnay, through Oyne by Mill of Buchanstone, and along the railway a few yards north of Oyne Station and Church, and falling into the Ury on the borders of the parishes of Oyne and Chapel of Garioch in the woods of Logie Elphinstone. It is very inter-

esting to learn from the church records of Oyne that
a collection was made in that Church in 1671 to repair
the bridge over the Gadie. This bridge was known as
"Sey's," and was rebuilt in 1836 close to the junction
of the Gill Burn with the Gadie.

The following is believed to be the oldest version
(author unknown) of

O ! GIN I WAR WHAUR GADIE RINS.

O ! gin I war whaur Gadie rins,
Whaur Gadie rins, whaur Gadie rins ;
O ! gin I war whaur Gadie rins
    At the back* o' Bennachie.
I never wad seek back again,
Seek back again, seek back again ;
I never wad seek back again
    To bide in the laigh countrie.

I never had but twa richt lads,
But twa richt lads, but twa richt lads ;
I never had but twa richt lads,
    An' it's dearly they loo'd me.
The tane was killed in Lowran Fair,
In Lowran Fair, in Lowran Fair ;
The tane was killed in Lowran Fair,
    An' the ither was drooned in Dee.

O ! wasna that twa dowie days,
Twa dowie days, twa dowie days ?
O ! wasna that twa dowie days,
    Twa dowie days for me ?
Instead o' buyin' my bridal dress,
My bridal dress, my bridal dress,
Instead o' buyin' my bridal dress,
    I bocht linen to bury them wi'.

---

* The "back" is the north side; so called from getting less
sun than the south.

They crooded on sae thick on him,
Sae thick on him, sae thick on him,
They crooded on sae thick on him,
    He could neither fecht nor flee.
But had he gotten man for man,
Man for man, man for man,
But had he gotten man for man,
    Or yet a man for three ;

He wadna lain sae low this day,
Sae low this day, sae low this day,
He wadna lain sae low this day,
    Aneath yon arne tree.
'Twas bluidy han's an' cruel hairts,
An' cruel hairts an' cruel hairts,
'Twas bluidy han's an' cruel hairts,
    That gart my Jamie dee.

O ! gin I war whaur Gadie rins,
Whaur Gadie rins, whaur Gadie rins,
O ! gin I war whaur Gadie rins,
    At the back o' Bennachie.
I'll seek his grave on Gadie side,
On Gadie side, on Gadie side,
I'll seek his grave on Gadie side,
    Syne lay me doon an' dee.

The more common and most poetic version is
attributed by some to Rev. John Park, D.D., of
St. Andrews, but others ascribe it to Rev. Mr. Barclay,
who was parson of Cruden some two hundred years
ago.   It runs thus :

Oh ! an' I were whaur Gadie rins,
'Mang blooming heaths and yellow whins,
Or brawlin' down the bosky linns
    At the back o' Bennachie.

Ance mair to hear the wild bird's sang,
To wander birks and braes amang,
Wi' friends and fav'rites left sae lang,
    At the back o' Bennachie.

How mony a day in blythe spring time,
How mony a day in summer's prime,
I've saunterin' wiled awa' the time,
    On the heights o' Bennachie.

Ah ! fortune's flowers wi' thorns grow rife,
An' walth is won wi' toil and strife—
Ae day gie me o' youthful life
    At the back o' Bennachie.

Ah, Mary, there on ilka nicht,
When baith our hearts were young and licht,
We've wandered by the clear moonlicht,
    Wi' speech baith fond and free.

Oh ! ance, ance mair whaur Gadie rins,
Whaur Gadie rins, whaur Gadie rins,
Oh ! might I dee whaur Gadie rins,
    At the back o' Bennachie.

The following is the version which has been traditionally ascribed to Dr. Arthur Johnstone, of New
Leslie, in the parish of Leslie. Johnstone was a
Guild Burgess of Aberdeen, and there are two portraits of him—one in Marischal College, dated 1623,
and another in King's College, dated 1629 :

Oh ! gin I war where Gadie rins,
Where Gadie rins, where Gadie rins,
Oh ! gin I war where Gadie rins
    At the back o' Bennachie.

I wad ne'er seek hame again,
Seek hame again, seek hame again,
I wad ne'er seek hame again
    To view my ain countrie.

For it's there the bonnie lassie lives,
The lassie lives, the lassie lives,
For it's there the bonnie lassie lives
    Wha's promised to be mine.

An' I'll buy to her the silken hose,
The silken hose, the silken hose,
An' I'll buy to her the silken hose,
    To deck her ankles fine.

An' a gowden band sall belt her waist,
Sall belt her waist, sall belt her waist,
An' a gowden band sall belt her waist,
    Wi' a diamond clasp to bind.

An' I'll braid her hair o' the chestnut hue,
The chestnut hue, the chestnut hue,
An' I'll braid her hair o' the chestnut hue,
    As it waves in the summer wind.

Wi' the rose sae red, and the rose sae white,
The rose sae red, and the rose sae white,
Wi' the rose sae red, and the rose sae white,
    For she's to be my bride.

An' syne awa' to the kirk they've gane,
To the kirk they've gane, to the kirk they've gane,
An' syne awa' to the kirk they've gane,
    Where they stood side by side.

An' the bands were tied, an' the blessin' said,
An' the blessin' said, an' the blessin' said,
An' the bands' were tied, an' the blessin' said,
    An' a happier pair than they

You wadna hae seen where Gadie rins,
Where Gadie rins, where Gadie rins,
You wadna hae seen where Gadie rins,
    In a lang, lang summer day.

The last version is by John Imlah, an Aberdeen
poet. He was born in North Street, Aberdeen, in
1799, and died in Jamaica in 1846 :

O ! gin I were where Gadie rins,
Where Gadie rins, where Gadie rins,
O ! gin I were where Gadie rins,
    By the foot o' Bennachie.

I've roamed by Tweed, I've roamed by Tay,
By Border Nith and Highland Spey,
But dearer far to me than they
    Are the braes o' Bennachie.

When bud and blossom sprout in spring,
And gar the birdies wag their wing,
They blithely bob, and soar, and sing,
    By the foot o' Bennachie.

When simmer cleeds the varied scene
Wi' licht o' gowd and leaves o' green,
I fain wad be, where aft I've been,
    At the foot o' Bennachie.

When autumn's yellow sheaf was shorn,
And a' the yards were fu' o' corn,
'Twas blithe to hear the clyack horn
    At the foot o' Bennachie.

When winter winds blaw sharp and shrill,
O'er icy burn and sheeted hill,
The ingle neuk is gleesome still
    At the foot o' Bennachie.

Though few to welcome me remain,
Though a' I loved be dead and gane,
I'll back, though I should live alane,
    To the back o' Bennachie.

Oh ! ance mair, ance mair where Gadie rins,
Where Gadie rins, where Gadie rins,
Oh ! lat me dee where Gadie rins,
    At the foot o' Bennachie.

CHAPTER X.

ITS NEIGHBOURS.

Bennachie is so situated that an uninterrupted view of it can be had from nearly every point of the compass, the neighbouring summits being comparatively few, as well as low in elevation. East and north there is a considerable stretch of low country with nothing to shut out the view—especially from the eastward ; while the near hills to the south are all considerably lower than Bennachie, and do not rise close to its base. About eight miles away to the north-west are the Foudland Hills, of slate quarry fame ; some thirteen miles to the west-north-west is the famed Tap o' Noth ; to the west, about nine miles off, are the Coreen Hills, beyond which may be seen the Buck of the Cabrach.

The "neighbours," however, I wish more particularly to refer to are none of these just mentioned, but are several nearer ones of a lesser order. They are Cairn William to the south, and Hart Hill, Parnassus, Candle Hill, Dunnideer, Christ's Kirk Hill, and the Hill of Tillymuick to the north, all of which can be easily seen from Bennachie, and, indeed, are in its immediate neighbourhood. Dunnideer, in particular, from its crowned summit, stands out prominently and, as it were, demands attention.

CAIRN WILLIAM.

Cairn William is the highest point (1469 feet) of the

range of hills known as the Menaway. It is south from Bennachie, on the opposite side of the Don, and is wooded nearly to the summit and very heathery, without any distinctive feature. The top nearest the Don is known as Pitfichie Hill (1244 feet), and has the remains of a felspar quarry, wrought for some time by an agent of the Staffordshire Potteries, but finally abandoned about 1835, chiefly, it is said, from the cost of the twenty miles' land carriage to Aberdeen, from which the stones, broken small and packed in casks, were shipped to England. A laird of Cluny is reported to have shod a horse with silver, the ore of which was found in the neighbourhood. On the north shoulder of Cairn William is the farm of Cairnabo. There is a tradition that James V. paid it a "surprise" visit in the garb of a "gaberlunzie man." He received but little entertainment on his arrival, as all the corn had been "frosted," but the guidwife, suspecting in the morning who the beggar-guest was, sung a sheep's head with the tongs for him. The King declared it to be the finest he had ever eaten, but said the place should rather be called Cornlessbo than Cornabo ! The oak chair used by the King on the occasion is still in existence, and it may be mentioned that a portion of what formed the carved panelling of the back is in the writer's possession. "John Duncan, weaver and botanist," lived at Cornabo for some years.

HART HILL.

This knoll—it scarcely deserves the name of hill—is 416 feet in height, and may be seen on the left as Oyne Station is neared from the south. It is about half-a-mile north-west of Harthill Castle, and is crowned

by the Church of Oyne, built in 1806. There is a
local saying that fully describes its situation :

> The Kirk o' Een, it stan's its lane,
> Upon a hill o' whun an' breem.

" Een" is the local pronunciation of Oyne, the meaning of which is very doubtful, but it is most likely
derived from the Gaelic. Formerly, the church was
situated at a lower elevation, in the churchyard in the
Kirktown, a little south of the present building, on the
site of St. Ninian's Chapel. When the churchyard
was recently improved and enlarged, a good few old
copper coins were found about the foundations of the
old church, almost every trace of which is now removed. A famous parson of Oyne was the "Priest's
giett" of John Knox, John Leslie by name. He was
the illegitimate son of the minister of Kingussie, who
was also illegitimate, and descended from the Leslies
of Balquhain. This John Leslie became a Judge in
the Court of Session as well as Bishop of Ross, and
the trusted councillor of Queen Mary.

When the kilt was proscribed after the rebellion of
1745, a stalwart man, Brodie by name, stuck faithfully
to it, especially on Sundays, making a point of attend-
ing the church of Oyne in full Highland dress in de-
fiance of the law. At last his persistence got so ob-
noxious to the authorities that, other measures failing,
half-a-dozen soldiers were sent from Inverurie to ap-
prehend him. They lay in wait for him one Sunday
as he left the church—the church being then in the
churchyard—and seized him as he came out. In an
instant, however, he shook himself free from the two
who held him by the arms, knocked them down, seized
a musket, and laid about him to such effect that he

quickly disabled or put the soldiers to flight. But this naturally rendered him such an object of interest that he had to conceal himself on Bennachie, where, however, he was attended to by the natives. After an enforced retirement of three weeks he succeeded in getting to the Continent, where he fought as a soldier for several years. Ultimately, in less troublous times, he returned to his native country.

PARNASSUS.

Parnassus (over 500 feet) is the little wooded hill a short way to the north-west of Oyne Station, on the slope of which may be seen Petmathen House. One of the lairds of Westhall (John Horn) called the little eminence his " Parnassus," and that name it has since retained, but the ancient name of the hillock was Knockdiddart. This laird had a reputation of his own, and built a two-roomed house on the top of Parnassus, which he is said to have used for immoral purposes—a statement so far borne out by the Oyne kirk-session records. He treated the " session " summonses very contemptuously, and was, moreover, a bit of a wag. A woman of rather a witch-like appearance, on being accused as a witch, repaired to Westhall and asked John if she looked like a witch. His reply was, " Indeed, woman, you look nae weel." Thoroughly disheartened the poor woman left, and bewailed with her crones her unfortunate looks. On their advice, however, she returned to Westhall, this time with silver in her hand, and again asked the laird's opinion (he was an advocate) of her looks, which was now considerably modified, for he replied, " Faith, lassie, you look nae sae ill as last time."

K

CANDLE HILL.

Candle Hill is close to, and immediately to the west of, Parnassus. It is locally pronounced " Can'le Hill," and is 670 feet in height. The lower part, towards the railway, rejoices in the name of Scabbed Craig. There was formerly a small lochlet on the top, and there is still a stone circle to the north-west. It is said to have derived its peculiar name from lights having been seen on it like "corpse-candles," already referred to, which are really the *ignis fatuus*. It appears chiefly in marshy places, or near stagnant waters, or in churchyards, and is generally supposed to be produced by the decomposition of animal or vegetable substances, and the evolution of gases which spontaneously inflame in the atmosphere. It is popularly known by such names as Will-o'-the-Wisp, Jack-o-Lantern, and Corpse-Candle.

DUNNIDEER.

Dunnideer (876 feet) is in the parish of Insch, between three and four miles north-west of Hermit Seat. Though its height is inconsiderable, it is pretty steep, and altogether it has a striking appearance, and is easily known from the summit having on it the remains of an old castle wall with a large window-like opening. On the top there are also the remains of a vitrified fort of considerable dimensions, and of much greater antiquity than the castle. Indeed, the belief is not unreasonable that Dunnideer was once a Pictish capital. The base of the hill is about two miles in circumference. So golden rich, says an old historian, was the pasturage that sheep fed on it had their teeth discoloured with gold! Fort and castle are both so ancient that there is no reliable account of the building of either, but it can yet be seen that the process of vitrification had been employed. One tradition says that King Gregory built the castle in the fourteenth century, but more than likely it is of much older date. Another tradition says that the castle was supplied with water by a pipe from the Foudland Hills, which was cut during a siege, and thus compelled a surrender.

CHRIST'S KIRK HILL.

The Hill of Christ's Kirk (1021 feet) is to the south-west of and separated from Dunnideer by the narrow valley of the Shevock, a tributary of the Ury, their tops being only about three-quarters of a mile apart. The railway and the Huntly turnpike run alongside the Shevock between the two hills. Christ's Kirk (or Rathmuriel) was of old a separate parish, but now forms part of Kennethmont. The burial ground is on the south-eastern slope of the hill, and the remains of a church may yet be seen. Near the church a market was at one time held *at night* in the month of June, which was known by the name of Christ's Fair or Sleepy Market. Ultimately the excesses committed at the market induced the authorities to change it from night to day; but so strongly were the people wedded to the old way that they did not take kindly to the new, and soon the market ceased to exist altogether. The adjacent farm is still called Sleepytown. This is, on very credible authority, believed to be the scene of the poem traditionally ascribed to James I., though there is no reason to believe that James I. ever wrote a line of it, and internal evidence alone would seem to prove that the authorship was much more local than even the south of Scotland. The following is the first stanza of *Chryst's Kirk on the Green:*

> Wes nevir in Scotland hard nor sene
> > Sic dansing nor deray,
> Nowther at Falkland on the grene,
> > Nor Pebilis at the Play,
> As wes of wowaris, as I wene,
> > At Christis Kirk on ane day.
> Thair came our Kitties weshen clene,
> > In their new kirtilis of gray,
> > > Full gay,
> At Christis Kirk of the grene that day.

HILL OF TILLYMUICK.

This hill, which has a height of 834 feet above sea level, is in the parish of Premnay, about half-a-mile south-east of the Church, and two-and-a-half miles north-west of the Mither Tap. It is a very near neighbour of Bennachie, being only about a mile northward of Hermit Seat. Its form is slightly conical with a flattish top, and it has rather an insignificant appearance. It is interesting, however, from having the remains of a rampart on the top which has a diameter of about 200 yards. This rampart, or circle of stones (which are of no great size), would appear to have had an entrance on the west side, though there are also openings on other sides, but evidently of modern date. Tillymuick means the sow's hill.

CHAPTER XI.

ITS CASTLES AND MANSIONS.

The castles and mansion-houses that surround and have an intimate connection with Bennachie are both numerous and interesting. One could easily be tempted to say a great deal on such a subject, but I have confined myself to such general facts as the Bennachie tourist would most probably care to learn concerning the historical buildings that are to be found at the foot of the hill. I will give them in their order as seen on going round the hill from near Inveramsay Station westward :—Balquhain Castle, Pitcaple Castle, Logie-Elphinstone House, Pittodrie House, Harthill

BALQUHAIN CASTLE.

Castle, Westhall, Petmathen House, Lickleyhead
Castle, Leslie Castle, Castle Forbes, Tillyfour House,
Pitfichie Castle, Monymusk House, Fetternear House,
and Tullos House. This list, it will be observed, contains no building that cannot claim connection, both
from neighbourhood and otherwise, with Bennachie.

BALQUHAIN CASTLE.

The picturesque ruined castle of Balquhain is on a
rocky knoll overhanging the Natrick Burn, in the
parish of Chapel of Garioch, about a mile east of the
church and three miles east from the Mither Tap.
The present building was erected in 1530, replacing a
more ancient structure burned by the Forbeses in
1526. In 1340 the lands of Balquhain were granted
by David II. to the Leslies. Queen Mary passed
a night in the castle on 9th September, 1562.
In 1746 it was ordered to be burned by the Duke
of Cumberland on his march to Culloden. There
is, however, a tradition that the Butcher Duke's
orders were not obeyed, the soldiers having been
bribed by one of the tenants with a bonnet full of
silver to set fire to damp straw only in the vault,
which caused sufficient smoke to have the appearance,
at a little distance, of the castle itself being burned.
More than three centuries before this another great army
had marched along by the foot of Bennachie, and we
fancy it would be difficult to say which was less wel-
comed by the inhabitants of the district. Near by,
on Gallow Hill, human skulls have been trenched up.

PITCAPLE CASTLE.

Pitcaple Castle may be seen on the right as Pitcaple
Station is approached from the south. It lies in the

hollow between the railway and the Ury, surrounded
by trees, and though not a fine building, is of considerable interest from a historical point of view.   In
1645 it was burned down, but was again rebuilt, though
about a hundred years ago it was once more in ruins,
and the then laird shared its occupancy with the jackdaws that lodged in the chimneys.   There is a local
saying, when an absurd tale is told, that " it is like
Pitcaple's angels—of the wrong colour," referring to a
descent of jackdaws one morning when the laird mistook them for angels.   But other visitors than jackdaws
have rendered this castle famous.   James IV. visited
it, and Mary Queen of Scots passed a night under its
roof (?) and planted a tree, still known as Queen
Mary's tree.   The next great personage known to have
stayed there—albeit compulsorily—was the Quaker
Provost of Aberdeen, Alexander Jaffray, who was a
member of Cromwell's Parliament.   He was arrested
in 1644 for his Covenanting principles.   " The great
Montrose" passed a night there in April, 1650, also compulsorily, having arrived as a prisoner, dressed in
mean, tattered garments, and his legs tied together by
straw ropes, riding on a pony, and thus balanced the
account.   He had been apprehended in Sutherland-
shire, and was detained in the castle a night on his
way to Edinburgh.   The laird's wife was his cousin,
and she offered him the means of escape, which he
declined, in case she might be compromised.   So the
beautiful story goes ; but another version has it that
he said he would rather take his chance in Edinburgh
than risk being smothered in the underground passage
offered as an exit !   The next Royal visitor was
Charles II. in July of the same year (1650), accom-

panied by the Dukes of Argyll and Buckingham, on his way south, after landing at Kingston-on-Spey. The laird, Leslie, on the day of the King's arrival, bought all the claret in St. Sair's Fair—a market still held near Insch—in order to make due provision for his Royal and noble guests. The story also says that, when Charles passed the Fair on his way to Pitcaple, he mistook the market tents for a Covenanting encampment, and accordingly gave them a wide berth! When Charles was at Pitcaple he remarked that a certain view in the neighbourhood reminded him of England. That part has since retained the name of England, and will be seen on the wayside when the traveller has crossed the railway bridge at Pitcaple on his way to Bennachie. On the opposite side of the Ury from the castle are the remains of a fort or camp, near to which the foundations of a bridge over the stream were come on recently. It is believed to be of Roman origin, as it lies in the probable line of march between the Peterculter and Auchterless Roman camps, and may have had some connection with the fort on the Mither Tap (*vide* page 28).

The present building, the work of an Edinburgh architect, mostly dates from 1830, and is the property of Colonel Lumsden of Pitcaple.

LOGIE-ELPHINSTONE HOUSE.

This is rather a plain building on the left bank of the Ury, in the parish of Chapel of Garioch, the oldest part of which dates from about 1690. It is a delightful residence, the only fault being the lowness of its situation. It faces the south, and has a fine lawn sloping to the Ury. There are some good portraits of various Elphinstones and Leslies in the house. Within the grounds are the ruins of the old church, disused since 1599, with the burial ground of Logie-Durno, near where

> Gadie wi' its waters fleet,
> Ury wi' its murmur sweet,
> They hae trysted aye to meet
> Among the woods o' Logie.

Another quotation from the Inverurie poet seems not very inappropriate here, though the reference is not to Logie-Durno Churchyard, but to one lower down on the other side of the Ury :

Far from her native Tay she sleeps, and other waters lave
The markless spot where Ury creeps around my Jeannie's grave.
Move noiseless, gentle Ury ! around my Jeannie's bed,
And I'll love thee, gentle Ury, where'er my footsteps tread.
For sooner shall thy fairy wave return from yonder sea
Than I forget yon lonely grave and all it hides from me.

PITTODRIE HOUSE.

This house is quite a mountain chateau, situated at a height of 685 feet on the north-eastern shoulder of the Mither Tap, about a mile and a half from the top, and with a wide view to the south. The ancient name of the estate was Balhaggardie, which has been over four hundred years in the possession of the same family, Knight-Erskine, descendants of the great house of Mar. Pittodrie House is beautifully placed among trees, with fine hollies and yews, in the parish of Oyne. The old house was burned in 1644 by Argyll's Covenanters.

HARTHILL CASTLE.

This ruin, known locally as Torries Castle, is in the parish of Oyne, on the left of the road as the Kirktown of Oyne is approached from the east. It is about a mile and a half north-east of Craig Shannoch, and is a massive building, with loop-holes, and it had formerly towers, turrets, &c., as became such a pretentious edifice. Now it is used as an implement storehouse by the neighbouring farmer (Torries), who kindly allows visitors the use of the key so that the interior may be inspected. It is stated to have been built in 1638, but an inscription on a stone, that had at one time been over the outer gate, would indicate that it had been erected before that date. The inscription runs :

1601 : K. J. Most Libera.

King James was in Aberdeen in 1601 ; and what more

likely than that he paid a passing visit, thus commemorated, to Harthill Castle?

The estate of Harthill was granted by Robert the
Bruce, about 1315, to an Abercromby of Birkenbog.
It afterwards passed, with additions, to the Leiths, but
was ultimately broken up, Harthill now forming part
of the estate of Pittodrie. The last Leith who possessed the lands is said to have set fire to the castle,
as stated in a previous chapter. One account says :—
"On the 15th of August, 1644, Sir William Forbes
went to the Castle of Harthill, in the Garioch, the seat
of John Leith, who was prisoner in Edinburgh, and,
taking his lady, children, and domestics, tied them to
the gates of the castle and shot them."

The superiority of St. Lawrence Fair (Lowran
Fair), referred to in Chapter I., formerly belonged to
the Leiths of Harthill. The market was (and is still)
held at Old Rain, in the parish of Rayne, and was
once of such importance that it lasted three days.
The Leiths raised the market dues payable to them to
such an exorbitant extent that in 1606, as the Aberdeen Burgh records show, the Aberdonians and others
summoned the superiors to the Court of Session on
the subject. The Fair is also mentioned in a ballad
already quoted, but it may be as well here to give the
first and last verses of another ballad :

> " Oh, minnie, I'm gaun to Lowran Fair."
> " Oh, Jamie, fat are ye gaun tae dee there ?"
> " Tae buy some harrow-graith an' some bowes,
> Tae strike up a pleuch in Ba'cairns knowes."
>
> .   .   .   .   .   .
>
> There sits a man on Ba'cairn's knowes,
> Wi' legs as crookit as twa ousen bowes ;
> 'T wad set him far better tae be herdin' at yowes,
> Than fermin' the hawdin' o' bonny Ba'cairn.

A noted foot o' Bennachie ballad-singer of the last century, Charles Lesly, believed to be an illigitimate son of the laird of Pitcaple, died at Old Rain in 1792, aged 105 years. He was better known as "Mussel Mou'd Charlie," and was quite a character. A small collection of ballads sung by him was published in Edinburgh in 1827, under the title of "The Ballad Book," with a small woodcut of Charlie under the title. The collection, I understand, is now very scarce (only a very small edition having been printed), and exceedingly valuable, so the chorus and middle verses, as rendered by Charlie, of the ballad just quoted, may also be given :

Chorus—Quhilk o' ye lasses will go to Buchairn ?
Quhilk o' ye lasses will go to Buchairn ?
Quhilk o' ye lasses will go to Buchairn ?
And be the guidwife o' bonnie Buchairn ?

I'll get a thiggin' frae auld John Watt,
And I'll get ane frae the Lady o' Glack,
And I'll get anither frae honest John Gray
For keeping his sheep sae lang on the brae.

" Lassie, I am gaun to Lowren Fair."
" Laddie, what are ye gaun to do there ?"
" To buy some ousen, some graith, and some bowes,
To plenish the toon o' Buchairn's knowes."

The castle had likely received its name from Hart Hill, a little to the north-west, and which had been probably so named from the deer then on Bennachie.

WESTHALL.

This is a very ancient mansion about half-a-mile north of Oyne Station, the grounds being finely wooded. According to Buchanan it was the Aberdeen diocesan residence in the 13th century. It came into

the family of Horn in the 17th century, and remained
in their possession for a considerable period. The
Dalrymples and Elphinstones ultimately acquired the
estate, but now Westhall belongs to General Disney
Leith. Round about the house are some fine old trees
and many fine yews and holly hedges. John, the last

WESTHALL.

of the Horns of Westhall, improved and ornamented
the grounds with trees, and was buried in a
coffin made from timber of his own planting. In
1570 the laird was John Abercromby, incumbent of
Oyne, Premnay, and Logie Durno. His predecessor
in Oyne Church was John Leslie, referred to in last
chapter.

PETMATHEN HOUSE.

This mansion, formerly known as Pitmedden House
(doubtless *Petmathen* is the more correct and ancient

spelling), has been considerably enlarged and practically rebuilt by the present proprietor, Major Thomas
Leith.   It is close to and on the north-west of Oyne
Station, and is finely situated among young plantations
on the south eastern slope of Parnassus, on the left
bank of the Gadie.   Looking at it, and the fine
grounds intersected by the Gadie, especially that part
between the Gadie and the railway, one can scarcely
believe that there stood the Westhall Flax Works,
erected in 1854.   Not a trace of them can now
be seen by the casual observer, though in the village
of Oyne gas-fittings may still be noticed, that speak of
the time when the houses in the vicinity were lighted
by gas produced at the Flax Works.   The Free Church,

LICKLEYHEAD CASTLE.

also, has the unmusical bell that called the workers together.

It may be interesting to note that the first laird of Pitmedden House was an Oyne "loon," who left the Garioch for Aberdeen, there to make his fortune. When he started for Aberdeen, besides the clothes on his back, all his belongings are said to have been half-a-crown, a shirt, and a pair of stockings.

LICKLEYHEAD CASTLE.

Lickleyhead Castle is about a mile and a quarter north-north-west of Black Hill, and is in the parish of Premnay, on the right bank of the Gadie. It formerly belonged to the Forbeses of Leslie, who bought it from Patrick Leith of Edingarioch, and was the seat of the lairds of Premnay. Now it belongs to the Lumsdens of Clova. The Leslies are the oldest family represented in the Garioch, the Leiths ranking after them in that respect. The building dates from 1609, but was considerably enlarged in 1876. Over the door is the inscription JF.MS 1629.

LESLIE CASTLE.

This picturesque ruin is in the parish of Leslie, on the left bank of the Gadie, nearly three miles north-westward of the top of Black Hill. It received its name from the ancient family of Leslie, who originally possessed the most of the land in the parish. From the Leslies the property passed to the Forbeses of Monymusk, one of whom, in 1661, considerably improved the castle. The estate is now in the possession of the Leith-Hays of Leith-hall, having been sold to the laird of Leith-hall by the last of the Leslie Forbeses in the end of the seventeenth century. Over

the door of the Castle is the inscription—" Hæc
Corp. Sydera Mentem." The old family of Leslie
is now represented by the Earl of Rothes.

CASTLE FORBES.

Castle Forbes, situated on the left bank of the Don,
on the south-west shoulder of Bennachie, in the parish
of Keig, is quite a modern building, having been
designed by the late Archibald Simpson, the Aberdeen
architect. It is a grand structure, built on a site
formerly known as Putachie, or Putarchy, according
to another authority, who also gives the old name as
Drimminor. It is the seat of the premier baron of
Scotland, Lord Forbes. The grounds round the
castle are extensive; within them are the remains of
an old church and a graveyard.

TILLYFOUR HOUSE.

The House of Tillyfour, or Place of Tillyfour, as it
is sometimes called, is on the left bank of the Don, in
the parish of Oyne, little over a mile south-west of the

top of the Millstone Hill. It has been greatly enlarged and improved by the present proprietor, (Mr. F. R. Gregson). The original building was a very old one, and belonged to the Earls of Mar. Latterly it passed into the hands of the Baronets of Monymusk, and then became so dilapidated that it was used as a byre.

PITFICHIE CASTLE.

The ruins of this castle are on the south side of the Don, about a mile north-westward from the village of Monymusk, on the west side of the road that winds round Pitfichie Hill. It now forms part of the estate of Monymusk, to which indeed it anciently belonged. It was for some time in the possession of the Chalmers family, and from them it passed to the family of Hurry or Urrie. The last laird of that name, Sir John Urrie, was a general in the Covenanting army, and was defeated by Montrose at Auldearn and Alford in 1645. After the latter defeat he retired with his broken forces to Pitfichie, where several of his wounded died and were buried in the vicinity. Several of their bodies have been found lately. On his way north he plundered Harthill Castle (Oyne). General Urrie turned his coat several times, but to little advantage ultimately, for he was hanged at Montrose in 1650 while in the Royal service. He was first a Royalist, then a Covenanter, and then, thinking the Covenanting cause hopeless, a Royalist again.

William Forbes, the young laird of Monymusk, married, about the end of the seventeenth century, Lady Jean, the eldest daughter of the first Earl and Countess of Kintore, the young couple residing at

L

Pitfichie Castle.   The following verses are all that remain of a ballad about this Lady Jean :

" Hoo dee ye like Pitfichie,
    Hoo like ye there to dwall ;
Hoo dee ye like Pitfichie,
    Gentle Jean o' Keith-hall ?"

" Oh, weel I like Pitfichie,
    An' I like there to dwall ;
Oh, weel I like Pitfichie,
    But nae half sae weel's Keith-hall."

" Oh, ye'll get wine an' wa'nuts,
    An' servants aye at yer call,
An' young Monymusk to dawt ye ;
    Ye had na that at Keith-hall."

" Oh, I had wine an' wa'nuts,
    An' servants aye at my call,
An' the bonny Laird o' Fyvie
    To see me at Keith-hall."

A ghost, with a red night-cap, was believed to run round the walls of the castle, but in recent years it has somehow failed to put in an appearance.

MONYMUSK HOUSE.

Monymusk House is a rather plain building, prettily situated on the right bank of the Don among trees. It dates from the Reformation, and, indeed, it is said that it was partly built from the materials of the old Priory of Monymusk, these being " seized " in the ordinary way.   Near the site, about half-a-mile east, Robert the Bruce encamped previous to the Battle of Barra (1308).   It is now the property of the Baronets (Grant) of Monymusk, but originally belonged to the Corsindae branch of the great family of the Forbeses.

FETTERNEAR HOUSE.

Fetternear House may be seen as the tourist crosses the Don from Kemnay Station. It belonged of old to the Bishops of Aberdeen, being one of their summer residences, having been built so far back as 1329 by Alexander Kininmonth, Bishop of Aberdeen. Near it a church was built in 1109, and strangely enough a new chapel of the old denomination (in addition to an unconsecrated erection) has recently been built near the site of the old one. There is a tradition that its predecessor was built near Bennachie, but that the walls sank every night to the level of the foundations, and accordingly it received the name of "Chapel o' Sink." The house, which is on the left bank of the Don, is the residence of the Leslies of Balquhain, who have considerably enlarged and beautified the grounds. Sir William Wallace visited Fetternear in 1297.

TULLOS HOUSE.

The ruins of Tullos House are about a mile and a-half south of Pittodrie House, and nearly the same distance east of the Mither Tap, from which they are visible. It was a comparatively small house of two storeys, with three gables, and an additional building at one of the corners. The latter part is now only a few feet above ground, but quite recently stood at a considerable height. Alexander Leslie of Tullos, often called "the guidman of Tullos," became, in 1671, Count Leslie of Balquhain.

CHAPTER XII.

ITS GEOLOGY AND BOTANY.

GEOLOGY.

The mass of Bennachie is granite, "often a reddish-brown binary compound of quartz and felspar, both, especially the latter, in regular crystals, well seen in drusy cavities. . . The summit of the hill is a good example of the mode in which granite decomposes, being built up as it were of oblong blocks, some placed horizontal, others inclined or vertical." (Nicol's Geology of Scotland). Percolating water and frost along the parallel lines of the joints which traverse the granite and split them open. According to the Geological Survey of Scotland, Bennachie is composed of granite, surrounded on the north side by diorite, on the east by gneiss, on the south by granite, and on the west by mica schist and knotted schist. The granite is not sufficiently close grained to suit fine work, more especially in polishing; nor is the colour equal to that of the finer red granites of Aberdeenshire. Consequently, although "Bennachie stanes" have been in request in the district surrounding the hill for door lintels and corners in building ever since the era of turf and "heather and dub" dwellings came to an end, granite quarrying has never been extensively carried on at any part of the hill.

BOTANY.

The following list, drawn up by Mr. W. S. Duncan,

formerly of Old Meldrum, gives a very fair idea of the Flowering Plants and Ferns to be found on Bennachie. With the botanical name I give also in each case the common name of the plant :

Anemone nemorosa (wood anemone).

Ranunculus flammula (small spearwort).

R. repens (creeping crowfoot).

R. acris (upright meadow crowfoot).

Corydalis claviculata (white climbing corydalis).

Cardamine pratensis (common bitter cress).

Viola palustris (marsh violet).

V. canina (dog's violet).

Drosera rotundifolia (round leaved sun-dew).

Parnassia palustris (grass of Parnassus).

Polygala vulgaris (common milk-wort).

Sagina procumbens (procumbent pearl-wort).

S. subulata (awl-leafed pearl-wort).

Stellaria uliginosa (bog stitch-wort).

Cerastium viscosum (narrow-leaved mouse-eared chickweed).

Hypericum pulchrum (small upright St. John's wort).

Linum catharticum (purging flax).

Oxalis Acetosella (common wood-sorrel).

Ulex Europæus (whin).

Genista Anglica (needle gorse or petty-whin).

Sarothamnus scoparius (common broom).

Trifolium repens (white clover).

Lotus corniculatus (common bird's-foot trefoil).

Orobus tuberosus (tuberous bitter-vetch).

Potentilla Tormentilla (tormentil cinque-foil).

Rubus Idæus (common raspberry).

R. Chamæmorus (mountain bramble or cloudberry).

Rosa villosa (villous or soft-haired rose).

R. canina (dog rose).

Pyrus aucuparia (rowan-tree).

Epilobium tetragonum (square-stalked willow-herb).

E. palustre (marsh willow-herb).

E. alpinum (Alpine willow-herb).

Montia fontana (water blinks).

Sedum villosum (hairy stonecrop).

Ribes grossularia (common gooseberry).

Lonicera Periclymenum (common honeysuckle or woodbine).

Galium verum (yellow bed-straw).

G. saxatile (smooth heath bed-straw).

G. palustre (white water bed-straw).

G. uliginosum (rough marsh bed-straw).

Scabiosa succisa (devil's-bit scabious).

Bellis perennis (common daisy).

Solidago Virgaurea (common golden-rod).

Achillea Ptarmica (sneeze-wort yarrow).

A. millefolium (common yarrow).

Senecio sylvaticus (wood groundsel or ragwort).

S. Jacobæa (common ragwort).

S. aquaticus (marsh ragwort).

Gnaphalium sylvaticum (Highland cudweed).

Carduus lanceolatus (spear-plume thistle).

C. palustris (marsh-plume thistle).

Centaurea nigra (black discoid knap-weed).

Hypochæris radicata (long-rooted cat's-ear).

Apargia autumnalis (autumnal hawkbit).

Leontodon Taraxacum (common dandelion).

Hieracium (hawkweed—three species).

Campanula rotundifolia (hairbell).

Vaccinium Myrtillus (blaeberry).

V. Vitis Idæa (red whortleberry or cranberry of this district, but not the true cranberry, which is the species *V. oxycoccos*).

Calluna vulgaris (common ling or cat-heather).

Erica Tetralix (cross-leaved heath).

E. cinerea (fine-leaved heath).

Arctostaphylos Uva-ursi (red bear-berry).

Ilex aquifolium (common holly).

Myosotis repens (creeping water-scorpion grass).

Digitalis purpurea (purple foxglove).

Serophularia nodosa (knotted figwort).

Melampyrum pratense (common yellow cow-wheat).

Pedicularis sylvatica (pasture louse-wort).

P. palustris (marsh louse-wort).

Rhinanthus Crista-Galli (common yellow-rattle).

Euphrasia officinalis (common eyebright).

Veronica officinalis (common speedwell).

V. serpyllifolia (thyme-leaved speedwell).

Prunella vulgaris (common self-heal).

Pinguicula vulgaris (common bitterwort).

Lysimachia nemorum (wood loose-strife).

Trientalis Europæa (European chickweed winter-green).

Plantago lanceolata (ribwort plantain).

Rumex aquaticus (grainless water-dock).

R. crispus (curled dock).

R. alpinus (alpine dock or monk's rhubarb).

R. Acetosa (common sorrel).

R. Acetosella (sheep's sorrel).

Empetrum nigrum (black crowberry).

Myrica gale (sweet bog myrtle).

Salix herbacea (least willow).

S. cinerea (grey sallow).

Orchis maculata (spotted palmate orchis).
Gymnadenia conopsea (fragrant gymnadenia).
Habenaria bifolia (butterfly habenaria).
H. albida (small white habenaria).
Listera cordata (heart-leaved tway-blade).
Goodyera repens (creeping goodyera).
Narthecium ossifragum (bog-asphodel).
Juncus acutiflorus (sharp-flowered rush).
J. lamprocarpus (shining-fruited rush)
J. uliginosus (lesser bog rush).
J. squarrosus (heath rush).
J. bufonius (toad rush).
J. effusus (common smooth rush).
J. conglomeratus (common rush).
Luzula sylvatica (great hairy wood-rush).
L. pilosa (broad-leaved hairy wood-rush).
L. campestris (field wood-rush).
Triglochin palustre (marsh arrow-grass).
Scirpus cæspitosus (early-stalked club-rush).
S. pauciflorus (few-flowered club-rush).
Eriophorum angustifolium (narrow-leaved cotton-grass).
E. vaginatum (hair-tail cotton-grass).
Carex dioica (diœcious carex or sedge).
C. pulicaris (flea carex).
C. stellulata (prickly-headed carex).
C. vulgaris (common carex).
C. panicea (pink-leaved carex).
C. pilulifera (round-headed carex).
C. flava (yellow carex).
C. binervis (green-ribbed carex).
C. glauca (glaucous heath carex).
Anthoxanthum odoratum (sweet-scented vernal grass).
Nardus stricta (common mat grass).

Agrostis canina (brown bent grass).

A. vulgaris (fine bent grass).

Holcus mollis (creeping soft grass).

H. lanatus (meadow soft grass).

Aira cæspitosa (tufted hair grass).

A. flexuosa (waved hair grass).

A. caryophyllea (silvery hair grass).

A. præcox (early hair grass).

Triodia decumbens (decumbent heath grass).

Poa annua (annual meadow-grass),

P. trivialis (rough meadow-grass).

Cynosurus cristatus (crested dog's-tail grass).

Festuca ovina (sheep's fescue-grass).

Polypodium vulgare (common polypody).

P. Dryopteris (tender three-branched polypody or oak fern).

P. Phegopteris (pale mountain polypody or beach fern).

Lastrea dilatata (prickly shield-fern).

L. Oreopteris (heath shield-fern).

L. Filix-mas (male shield-fern)

Athyrium Filix-fæmina (lady-fern).

Blechnum boreale (northern hard fern).

Pteris aquilina (common braken).

Hymenophyllum Wilsoni (Scottish filmy-fern).

Lycopodium clavatum (common club-moss).

L. alpinum (savine-leaved club-moss).

L. Selago (fir club-moss).

L. selaginoides (lesser alpine club-moss).

Equisetum sylvaticum (branched wood horsetail).

CHAPTER XIII.

THE BATTLE OF HARLAW.

Frae Dunideir as I cam' throuch,
  Doun by the hill of Banochie
Allangst the lands of Garioch,
  Grit pitie was to heir and se
  The noys and dulesum hermonie,
That evir that dreiry day did daw,
  Cryand the corynoch on hie,
    " Alas, alas, for the Harlaw."

The battle of Harlaw is the greatest event that has
ever taken place, at least in historic times, under the
shadow of Bennachie, and therefore the present
chapter fitly concludes the account of the mountain
of the Garioch.

Even in spite of the national importance of the
sanguinary contest on the field of Harlaw (anciently
Harelaw), and apart from its local interest, more particularly to Aberdonians, it is to be feared that comparatively few are exactly aware of the great issues that
were then at stake, or of the nature of the contending
forces engaged in that famous battle.

Harlaw is in the south-east part of the parish of
Chapel of Garioch, in the angle formed by the main
line of the Great North of Scotland Railway with its Oldmeldrum branch, and on the right (east), as Inveramsay
Station is approached from the south. It lies between
the two public roads that fork a little north-west of the
Burgh Muir of Inverurie, the one on the east leading

north through Daviot, the other being the main turnpike
to the north-west. On the west Harlaw is bounded by
the Ury, and is about two miles north-west of Inverurie,
fully a mile east from Inveramsay Station, and about
five miles east-north-east from the summit of the
Mither Tap of Bennachie. The site is easily discernible from the existence of "Harlaw House," with its
tower, which stands on the top of the broad elevation,
on and below which the battle raged.

> The cronach's cried on Bennachie,
> And doun the Don and a' ;
> And Hieland and Lawland may mournfu' be
> For the sair field of Harlaw.

The battle was fought on 24th July, 1411, on St.
James's even. As the old rhyme has it :

> Wast o' Inverury, aboot a mile or twa,
> On a bonny hillheid lies the toun o' Harlaw.
> July the twenty-fourth, St. James's even,
> Harlaw was foucht, fourteen hun're an' eleven.

The two generals were Donald, Lord of the Isles, in
command of the Highland forces, and Alexander, Earl
of Mar, the commander of the Royal army, the Duke
of Albany being then Regent of Scotland, as King
James I. was in captivity. The circumstance that
indirectly brought about the battle was simple enough,
but characteristic of the then turbulent times, the Regent
having appropriated the Earldom of Ross, which in
due course of events would have fallen in all probability to the Lord of the Isles. Donald promptly
took active steps in the assertion of his supposed
rights, and crossed over from Skye to Ross-shire, where
he was well received. Hector Maclean of Duart, his
nephew, was his lieutenant, and besides others of note

he had with him the chief of the Clan Macintosh. At Dingwall he met a slight temporary check, but soon pushed on to Inverness, gathering strength as he went. Then his advance was easy to Strathbogie and thence into the Garioch, in both of which districts he committed great excesses, probably thinking that, as they pretty much belonged to the Earl of Mar, he was only spoiling the Philistines. He now renewed an old threat to burn Aberdeen, and promised his hungry Highlanders a rich booty on the plunder of that city. This thoroughly frightened the Aberdonians, and at the same time put them on their mettle—and so, perhaps, Donald defeated his own purpose! He had perforce to call a halt in the Garioch, with what result will be seen directly.

The first verse of an old ballad says :

> As I cam' in by Dunnideer,
>   An' doun by Netherha',
> There were fifty thousan' Hielanmen,
>   A' marchin' to Harlaw.

Sir Walter Scott considerably reduces this number :

> They hadna ridden a mile, a mile,
>   A mile but barely ten,
> When Donald came branking down the brae
>   Wi' twenty thousand men.

A version of the "Netherha'" ballad sends up the numbers to, for the times, an impossible extent :

> Oot o' ninety thousan' men
>   Gaed hame but thirty-three ;
> An' oot o' saxty thousan' men
>   Gaed hame but fifty-five.

Donald having the 90,000, and Mar the 60,000. But the actual numbers engaged were, it is believed,

10,000 on the side of the Highlanders, and 1000 only on the Regent's side.

The Earl of Mar was commissioned by the Regent, his uncle, to raise forces to oppose the Lord of the Isles. In a short time Mar, who was a soldier of renown, found himself at the head of about a thousand men, gathered from the districts of Angus, Mearns, Mar, Formartine, Buchan, and Garioch. One can easily fancy that the inhabitants of these districts had become thoroughly alarmed at the advent of the Highland host, having good cause to fear the result should not Donald's southward march be stayed. There was certainly a great disproportion between the numbers of the opposing hosts, but when quality is considered they were pretty fairly matched. As Scott's ballad says, the Highlanders

> . . . hae but their tartan plaids,
> And we are mail-clad men.

In short, the Highlanders were little more than a fierce horde; while the Royalist army was largely made up of men of rank and position, well disciplined in arms. Of the men of local interest on the Regent's side only two need be mentioned here. They are thus referred to in the ballad first quoted :

> Gude Sir Alexander Irving,
> The much renownit laird of Drum.
>
> . . . .
>
> And Gude Sir Robert Davidson,
> Quha provost was of Aberdene.

From the names given in the Aberdeen Council Register of men appointed to do battle with the "Ketterines" at the time of the battle of Harlaw, 33 besides the Provost, went forth to face Donald and preserve their "braif toun" from the rapacious enemy. Likely enough personal safety, as much as a feeling of loyalty to King James, thus moved the Bon-Accord burgesses.

The Earl of Mar marched from Aberdeen with the main portion of his army, being joined at Inverurie by the more northerly contingent. From Inverurie he proceeded northward across the Ury, by the Braes of Balhaggardy, to the field of battle. There was no hesitation on his part in giving, and as little on the part of the Islesmen in accepting battle. No doubt Mar had duly considered the disproportion between his handful of men and the enemy, and had come to the conclusion that discipline, with personal valour and mail-clad knights with superior arms, would prevail against the half-naked multitude opposed to him. At all events he knew, as a brave and good soldier, that his duty was to prevent, at all hazards, Donald's further advance on what must have been practically a defenceless country. That the engagement would, in any event, be a severe one, Mar had doubtless fully reckoned, and had therefore disposed his little army to the best advantage.

The position of the field of battle did not give much scope for cavalry—a circumstance well present, doubt-less, in Donald's mind. The first onset must have been terrible, the Highlanders yelling and shouting, as their custom was, when coming up on their opponents. But the superior arms and discipline of the Royalists must have told terribly on them, and, had it not been for their numbers, there would soon have been an end of the fight by the defeat of the Islesmen. But as the Royalists broke in on them, dealing death and destruction with almost every sweep of their weapons, they were fastened on by the eager Celts—men also of great courage in battle—taking the place of their slain comrades, and their very numbers prevailed against the powerful foe. Thus, no sooner had Mar's forces overpowered those in their immediate vicinity than a fresh lot stood before them, ready to cut down the horses, and with their dirks to search out the weak spots in the harness of the Royalists. So the fight and the slaughter continued till nightfall. Then the Highlanders retired unpur sued, for the Royalist army was so reduced and weakened that the remnant could do nothing more than pass the night on the field, glad enough, it may be, to find next morning the enemy out of sight away to the north-west by Bennachie. Of the Highlanders one of the ballads thus speaks:

> And sic an a pilleucherie,
>   The like ye never saw,
> As was amang the Hielanmen
>   When they saw Macdonal fa'.

> And when they saw that he was deid,
>   They turned and ran awa' ;
> And they buried him at Leggat's Den,
>   A lang mile frae Harlaw.

But Donald did *not* fall in the battle, and it was not till the following year that the Regent was able to force him to a temporary subjection. The same ballad goes on to say :

> On Munonday at morning
>   The battle it began :
> On Saturday at gloaming
>   Ye'd scarce telt wha had won.

And sic a weary burying,
    The like ye never saw,
As there was the Sunday after that,
    On the muir down by Harlaw.

Gin ony body spier at ye
    For the men ye took awa';
They're sleeping soun' and in their sheen,
    I' the howe aneath Harlaw.

These statements are so far incorrect, for the battle lasted but a single day. However, they show the great hold the battle took on the minds of the people, and the importance attached to the result. The advance of civilisation rather than comparative barbarism was assured, and the Royal authority so far vindicated. Poetry and music alike kept up the memory of the fight.

The slaughter on both sides, as can easily be imagined, was very great, but naturally told most on the Royalists. On Donald's side the only men of rank that fell were Maclean and Macintosh; on Mar's side quite a host of notables were slain. The following only need be mentioned here:—Leslie of Balquhain (his castle looked up to the scene of the battle), and his six sons; Irvine of Drum; Gilbert of Greenlaw; and the Provost of Aberdeen. The body of the latter was taken to Aberdeen, and buried in the Town's Churchyard, where, when the West Church was repaired some three hundred years after, his grave was discovered. On the skull was a silk cap in good preservation. His reputed armour now stands in the Town-Hall. In the ruined kirk of Kinkell*, nearly

---

*A parson of Kinkell, Alexander Galloway, was the architect of the Bridge of Dee.

two miles to the south-east of Inverurie, may yet be seen a monumental record of the battle—the only such record in existence.   It is the upper half of the tombstone of Gilbertus de Greenlaw (Berwickshire).   This stone was believed to mark the grave of Scrimgeour, the Constable of Dundee, who also fell at Harlaw, till Mr. Jervise, of "Epitaphs and Inscriptions" fame, discovered, from the portion of the name left and the heraldic insignia, the name of the person really commemorated.   The stone is not entire, having been broken before 1592, when the opposite side was used to commemorate a laird of Ardmurdo !   The inscription now reads thus :

> HIC JACET : NOBILIS
> ARMIGER GILBERTUS DE GRIE
> ANNO   OM   .   M . CCCC . XI .

It is not without interest also to observe that William Tillidaff, one of the Rayne church vassals who fell in the battle, is legally recorded on account of his son having been served heir to him in 1413, in terms of an Act exempting heirs of those who fell at Harlaw from the feudal fines usually exacted on entering into possession of estates.

According to tradition, what is now known as Pley Fauld was the scene of the main part of the battle. Maclean's grave and Drum's cairn are both to be seen on the field, as well as the Liggar Stone, a whinstone monolith about seven feet in height, believed to mark the place where the women who followed the Highlanders were slain and buried.   Leggat's Den is so called, if tradition can be relied on, from a meeting once held there between a Papal legate and the King, and there,

M

perhaps, Macintosh was buried—certainly not Donald. Some fifty years ago, ashes, bones, and a stone coffin were found in two cairns that were opened; and in 1837 the tenant of the farm came, while trenching, on the bones of about a dozen bodies. Truly the battle of Harlaw is not without monuments in plenty; the concluding stanzas of the ballad quoted at the head of the chapter says :

> Thair was not, sin' King Keneth's days,
>   Sic strange intestine crewel stryf
> In Scotland sene, as ilk man says,
>   Quhair mony liklie lost thair lyfe ;
>   Quhilk maid divorce twene man and wyfe,
> And mony children fatherless,
>   Quhilk in this realme has bene full ryfe ;
> Lord, help these lands, our wrangs redress.
>
> In July, on Saint James his even,
>   That four-and-twenty dismall day,
> Twelve hundred, ten score, and eleven,
>   Of zeirs sen Chryst, the suthe to say ;
>   Men will remember as they may,
> Quhen thus the veritie they know,
>   And mony a ane may mourn for ay
> The brim battil of the Harlaw.

INDEX.

Dark figures (thus **46** denote the page referring more particularly to the subject.

	Page.
Aiken's Stane, Maggie, . .	33
Averon Knap, *vide* Moss Grieve.	
Back Burn, ...	16
,, o' Bennachie, . .	10, **129**
Ballad Lore, ...	61
Balquhain Castle, . 26, 141, **142**	
Baron's Cairn, ...	47
Basil Law, *vide* Law, Basil.	
Battle of Harlaw, . . ,10, **162**	
Bede House, . . . **27**, 90	
Beeches, The, ...	23
Bend-up-High, . . 11, **12**, 100	
Bennachie, *passim*.	
,, Articles of antiquity,	44
,, Back o', . . 10, **129**	
,, Bonnie (The) Lass o',	75
,, Boundaries of, . .	13
,, Burns of, . . .	15
,, Couplets on, . .	9
,, Distances to, . .	18
,, Extent of, . .	13
,, Height of, . .	12
,, Jock o', . . . 29, **61**	
,, Keys of, . . . 17, **64**	
,, Meaning of, . .	11
,, Moss reserved on, .	105
,, Origin of name, .	10
,, Routes to, . .	18
,, Situation of, . .	10
,, Spelling of, . .	11
,, Summits of, . .	12
,, Tops marked on O.S.	
Map, . . .	15
,, Wee, Wee Man o', .	73

	Page.
Berry Hill, ...	21
,, Pot, . . .	19
Beverley (Colonist), . . .	94
Birks Burn, . . . 15, 32, 90	
,, The, ...	59
Black Hill, ... 11, 14	
,, Knap, . . .	14
Blackwell Head, . . 15, 16	
Blue Hill, ...	47
Boddach Stone, . . . 90, **91**	
Bogend, ... 16, 20	
Bogie's Burn, ...	16
Bonnie Lass o' Bennachie, The,	75
Botany and Geology, Its, . .	156
Brackla Burn, ...	16
,, Hill, ...	14
Bridges over Don, . . .	127
Brodie and Kilt, . . .	136
Brow, The, ...	19
Bruntwood Tap, . 14, 16, **58**, 89	
Buck of Cabrach, . . 40, **41**, 134	
Cairnabo, ...	135
Cairncouly, ... 90, **91**	
Cairn-mon-earn, . . .	9
Cairn William, . . .	134
Candle Hill, ...	138
Castle Forbes, . . 12, 18, 123. **152**	
Castles and Mansions, Its, .	141
Cat Cairn, ...	47
Chapelcrook, ...	35
Chapel o' Sink, . . .	155
,, of Garioch. . .	26
Chie, ...	11
Christ's Fair, ...	139

	Page.
Christ's Kirk Hill, . . .	139
Clachie Burn, . 16, 29, 30, 32, 89, 90	
Clochnaben, . . . 9, 40, 41	
Cluny, Laird of, . . 108, 135	
Colonists, The, . . . 93, 107	
Colony, The, ... 93	
Commonty, The, . . . 88	
,, Beattie's Report on, 102	
,, Boundaries of, . 89	
,, Division of, . . 98	
Corrie Burn, ... 16	
,, Hill, . . , . 14	
Corryhabbie Hill, . . . 38, 40	
Couplets on Bennachie, . . 9	
,, Don, . . . 126	
,, Een, . . 22, 136	
,, Monymusk, . . 31	
Craiglaggan Burn, . . . 16	
Craignathunder, . . . 13, 90	
Craig Shannoch, . 11, 14, 25, 44	
Cullen's School, Lord, . . 35	
Cup-marked stone, . . . 30	
Dawson, Robert, . . . 41	
Deer, dun, ... 31	
,, red, ... 25	
,, roe, ... 25	
Delau Burn, ... 16	
Devil's Stane o' Kemnay, . . 29, 84	
Distance seen from heights, . 37	
Don, The, ... 125	
,, Bridges over, . . . 127	
Dorlethen (suicide), . . . 50	
Drimminor, ... 152	
Drumdurno, The Maiden of, . 117	
Duncan, John, ... 135	
Dun deer, ... 31	
Dunnideer, ... 134, 138	
East Top, vide Mither Tap.	
Een, Couplets on, . . 22, 136	
England, ... 144	
English Quarry, . . . 59	
Enzian, ... 34	
Eviction, An, ... 108	
Fairies, ... 124	
"Far from her native Tay she	
sleeps," 145	
Fetternear House, . . 29, 155	
Ferney How, ... 16	

	Page.
Fir Park, ... 23, 90	
Flax Works, ... 150	
Fore Burn, ... 16	
Foudland, Hills of, . . 25, 40, 134	
Gadie, The, ... 10, 128	
"Gadie wi' its waters fleet," . 145	
Garbit Burn, ... 16	
,, How of the . . 16, 89	
,, Tap, . . 14, 16, 58	
Garioch Ford, . . . 89, 91	
,, The, ... 122	
Geology, ... 156	
Giant of the Hill, . . . 61	
Giants, The Rival, . . . 63	
Gill Burn, . . 16, 19, 23, 25	
,, Well, ... 25, 45	
Gillree Burn, . . . 16, 21, 22	
Gills, ... 19	
Gilmore, Wm., ... 50	
Ginshie Burn, ... 16	
Gouk Stane, The, . . . 90, 91	
Greatstone, ... 29	
Grole o' the Garioch, The, . 123	
Gweel o' the Garioch, The, . 123	
Harlaw, Battle of, . . 10, 162	
Hart Hill, ... 135, 148	
Harthill Castle, . 20, 45, 67, 146, 153	
Harthill's Cave, ... 45	
Heather Brig, . . . 32, 90	
Hermit Seat, . . . 11, 14	
Hill Fort, The, . . 10, 47, 52	
,, Park, . . 23, 25, 124	
,, Well 21, 90	
"Hoo dee ye like Pitfichie," . 154	
Horn, John, . . . 137, 149	
Horndoyne, ... 20	
Hosie's Well, . . 21, 49, 50, 79	
How of the Garbit, . . 16, 89	
Hummel Craig, ... 14	
Inns, ... 18	
Inscription on Mither Tap, . 49, 98	
Jack, Jane, ... 51	
Jamieson, Wm., . . . 59, 95	
Jock o' Bennachie, . . 29, 61	
,, Noth, ... 61	
Jock's Sark, . . . 46, 61	
Kemnay, Route from, . . 29	
,, The Devil's Stane o' - 29, 84	

Page.

Kewlie Well, ... 30, 91
Knockdiddart, ... 137
Lady's Well, ... 30
Laing (suicide), ... 43
Lang Johnnie Moir, . . . 66
Lass o' Bennachie, The Bonnie, 75
Law, Basil, ... 23
Leith's House, ... 45
Leslie Castle, ... 151
Leslie, John, . . . 136, 149
Leslie of Balquhain, . . 47, 116
Leslie's Cross, ... 116
Lesly, Charles, ... 148
Lickleyhead Castle, . 16, 150, 151
Linn, The, ... 27
Little John's Length, . . 14, 61
   ,,   Man, The, . . . 73
   ,,   Oxen Craig, . . 14, 25
Logie-Elphinstone House, . 144
Lord Cullen's School, . . 35
Lowran Fair, . . . 24, 147
Maggie Aiken's Stane, . . 33
Maiden Castle, . . . 10, 28
   ,,   Causeway, . 10, 28, 47, 51
   ,,   Craig, . . . 49
   ,,   Stone, . . 10, 26, 110
Malt Burn, ... 94
March Burn, ... 16
Masonford, ... 20
Menaway Range, . . . 135
Middle Burn, ... 16
Mill of Tillyfour, . . . 36
Millstone Hill, . . 12, 15, 59, 89
Mither Tap, . 9, 10, 12, 13, 18, 46
Monymusk, Couplet on, . . 31
   ,,   House, . . . 31, 154
   ,,   Route from, . . 30
Moss Grieve, . . 14, 46, 107
Mussel Mou'd Charlie, . . 148
My Lord's Throat, . . . 32
"My Mither men't," &c. . . 27
Neighbours, Its, . . . 134
Nether Maiden, . 13, 14, 46, 49
Nether Tap, vide Mither Tap.
Nursery, The, ... 23
"O! Gin I war whaur Gadie Rins," 129
"Oh, minnie, I'm gaun to Lowran
   Fair," 147

Page.

Ord Mill, ... 31, 34
Ousen Craig, vide Oxen Craig.
Oxen Craig, . 11, 13, 14, 18, 39
Oyne, Church of, . . 23, 136
   ,,   Couplets on, . . 22, 136
   ,,   Route from, . . . 19
Paradise, ... 31
Parnassus, ... 137
Petmathen House, . . 137, 149
Pitcaple Castle, . . . 28, 142
   ,,   Fort, . . . 28, 144
   ,,   Route from, . . 26
Pitfichie Castle, . . 13, 31, 153
   ,,   Hill, ... 135
Pitgaveny, ... 16, 89
Pitmachie, ... 12, 24
Pitsligo, Lord, ... 48
Pittodrie House, . . 26, 145
Place of Tillyfour, . . . 152
Putachie, . . . 12, 123, 152
Quarry Hill, . . . 14, 16, 59
"Quhilk o' ye lasses will go to
   Buchairn?" 148
Ramstone Mills, ... 31
Red Deer, ... 25
Rival Giants, The, . . . 63
Robbie Deson's Tap, . . . 41
Robert Dawson, ... 41
Roe Deer, ... 25
Rushmill Burn, ... 15, 26
Ryehill Burn, ... 16
Scabbed Craig, ... 138
Scare Hill, ... 15
Scarfauld Hill, ... 15, 16
Selby, Hill of, ... 119
Shannoch Well, ... 25
Shiel Know, ... 15, 16
Sleepy Market, ... 139
Snowie, Mary, ... 96
Squatters, ... 92, 107
St. Lawrence Fair, . . 24, 147
St. Sair's Fair, ... 144
Star Bog Burn, ... 16
Stay Know, . . 14, 90, 107
Tap o' Noth, . . . 9, 61, 134
Thomas the Rhymer, . 17, 31, 126
Three Fords, The, . . . 20
Tillybrack, ... 15

	Page.		Page
Tillyfour House, . . .	152	Wallace, Sir William, .	30, 155
,, Mill of, . . .	36	Watch Craig, . . .	11, 14, 42
Tillymuick, Hill of, . . 14, 90,	140	Waterfall, ...	27
Tombeg, ...	32	Watt, Charles, ...	28
Tops, On the, ...	37	Wee, Wee Man o' Bennachie, .	73
Torries, *vide* Harthill Castle.		Westhall, ...	23, 148
Tullos House, . . 30,	155	,, Flax Works, . .	150
Turf Hill, ... 15,	89	Westhaugh, ... 32,	36
Upper Woodend, . . .	32	West Top, *vide* Oxen Craig.	
Ury Fort, ... 28,	144	Whitehouse, Route from, . .	18
View from Mither Tap, . .	49	Wolf's Stone, ...	30
,, Oxen Craig, . .	40	Woodend, ...	35
,, Watch Craig, . .	44	,, Upper, . . .	32

THE END.

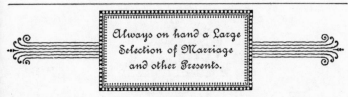

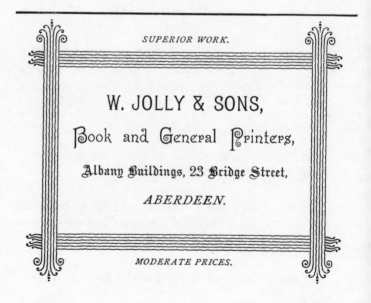

DEESIDE
HYDROPATHIC ESTABLISHMENT,
Heathcot, near Aberdeen.

THE Climate of Deeside is the most bracing in Britian.   Residents at this Establishment have the privilege of

Preserved Salmon & Trout Fishing in the River Dee,

as it runs through the Estates of Heathcot and Ardoe for a distance of two miles.

THE TURKISH AND OTHER BATHS
are constructed with all the latest improvements necessary for the practice of Hydropathy.

Terms per Week, £2 10s.; for Two having same Bedroom, £2 5s. each. From 1st November to 30th April, £1 15s.; and for Two in same room, £1 13s. 9d. each.

FOR PARTICULARS APPLY TO
Dr. STEWART, Medical Superintendent, Heathcot, near Aberdeen.

WILLIAM WALKER & SONS'
Unrivalled Teas.